Johannes & Eva-Maria Holmer

I Know God's Plan is Perfect

Lydia – a life full of trust

Translators:
Maria Päßler and Prof. Anne Schreiber

Cover Image:
Copyright © by Johannes Holmer

Editors:
Uta Mueller and Michael Lutz
Ocean of Minds Media House Ltd.
www.oceanofmindsmedia.com

Publisher:
Johannes Holmer
An der Kirche 1, 17166 Schorssow, Germany
www.holmer.de; johannes@holmer.de

Production and publishing: BoD - Books on Demand, Norderstedt
ISBN: 9783734712692

Content

Foreword for the English Edition

It has been more than 10 years ago now since we had to say goodbye to Lydia, who was known by many only as Puschel. Unfortunately, it took a while until we could publish an English translation of her book.

We have received much encouragement and gratitude over the years for publishing the German book. Often this was coupled with a report about new-found faith or a closer relationship with our Lord Jesus Christ. That was the main purpose of the German edition and is our hope for this edition as well. We were asked over and over again about an English edition of "I Know God's Plan is Perfect", especially by friends from Puschel's times in Holsbybrunn and San Salvador.

We hope for this book to be a blessing and give many young people new impulses to grow closer in their relationship with Jesus and communicate more intensely with Him.

We are always happy to hear about your personal experiences or encounters with Lydia. The bilingual internet homepage (www.puschel.holmer.info) still exists today. You will be able to find an e-mail address for personal messages if you wish.

We would like to thank all those who have made the English edition possible. Especially Maria Päßler, as well as Professor Schreiber (California) for final edits. We particularly thank the editors, Uta Müller and Michael Lutz, for preparing the publication of the English edition. Last, but not least, the final editing by Donna Schoon, Holsbybrunn, Sweden!

May God place His blessing on everything.

Eva-Maria and Johannes Holmer, December 2022

Foreword

What Makes a Person Great?

I ask myself this question often when I report on the great people of our time. Presidents, chancellors, ministers, or other such officers and dignitaries: they are found playing their part on the world stage, where at the beginning of the first act the applause is often deafening, but by the end, they are booed off the stage. They remain only as an historical side note in the margin of the memory of the general populace, depending on how much good or evil they caused and whether or not they made the headlines. Some may object and say the question of greatness is not the question to ask; instead, the balance of life is not so much about being historically great but much more about one's personal happiness.

According to this type of thinking, it is not the one who receives the most praise who wins, but the one who has the most toys, the one who has the most fun for the longest amount of time. In both questions of greatness and happiness, Lydia did not come out on top of the list of the historically famous. Compared to the popular standards of success, she was a little light that faded too quickly and left this world unnoticed.

Oh, but while she lived, she shone brightly! And how! She radiated so much that the hearts of those who knew her, mine included, still now and probably always will warm at the thought of her. She was seen as a superstar, a super nova, an exception.

Her life's glow neither reflected a life of comfort nor did it come from within, tied to her fleeting heartbeat. Instead, it came from God, who filled her life to the fullest. Because of this, she was right when she wrote a few years before the devastating cancer diagnosis, "I am very excited to see what God does with my life. I often notice that God does things we could never have imagined. Such a life is so exciting!"

In retrospect, just as easily as it came to me to purposely classify Lydia's life in God's plan of healing, it was equally as hard to accept her unspeakable suffering that led to her death. I questioned,

"Jesus, was that really necessary? How could you sit back and watch, while one of your most loyal disciples endured such excruciating pain as an aggressive growth devoured her body?" In the past, I have preached that companionship with Jesus can also mean we will suffer with Him, but in this specific case, this truth seemed simply too brutal and unfair.

The answer to the purpose of Lydia's battle with her health is one I will only receive once I am in heaven. What I do know is this. The cancer did not conquer her, but instead transformed her into an exquisite beauty. I have never – and *Lydia shone brightly* I write this totally without journalistic exaggeration – known a person who embodied the Christ-like virtues of faith, hope, and love better than Lydia, in spite of and because of her difficult fate.

When I visited her in Bülow, a great strength emanated from her room, not unlike that which one might expect from a chancellor's office. After every visit, I realized I was the one who had received a gift.

The depth of her faith, the confidence and friendliness that shone forth from Lydia, whether on crutches, in the wheelchair, or in the hospital bed, always had an effect on me. I am amazed how a creature whose life slowly drained from her body could appear so energetic, so thankful, so gracious.

It was not an accident that she named her little dog "Grace," for she stubbornly trusted God's grace and mercy, and with her life's example shamed many healthy Christians whose affluence and ease of life have washed away the substance of their faith.

She understood that God's grace and mercy aren't seen in the midst of circumstances of great health and worldly prosperity, but in the irreversible deliverance from earthly limitations and human suffering.

Twice I experienced a worship service with Lydia in her home church: first at Easter and then nine months later at her funeral. It comforts me to know that even though it is true she died, she isn't really dead. I know I will again see her blonde, curly head and her fiery, yet cheerful, eyes before this century is over, when it is my time to die.

Those inquiring as to whether Lydia was one of the great people of our time, or if her life was full of happiness, are essentially asking the wrong questions. Earthly happiness lasts but for a *She is now doing splendidly* moment, and we humans don't have the proper means to measure true greatness. Instead, the simple fact is that Lydia led a full life, and now, being in heaven, her joy has been made complete! She finished her biologically restricted and three-dimensionally limited existence with great endurance.

She brought a light into the world that makes all spotlights pale in comparison.

Thank you, Lydia – and thank you, Jesus.

Markus Spieker

One day I will die like everyone else. But I know for certain that I will experience a more beautiful world. Jesus has embedded this hope within me.

Lydia Holmer, before her death

Prologue

Farewell to Puschel

February 12, 2012. Wintry light pours through the church windows onto the 350 people solemnly dressed for the ceremony. They sit closely packed in the pews in the small village church of Bülow, which lies along Malchiner Lake. Because there aren't enough chairs, many have to stand at the back of the church. It doesn't bother them, however, and instead emphasizes the special nature of this service. In the middle of the church, a camera is set up on a tripod so this worship service can be watched live on the internet all around the world, enabling another 300 people to be present.

Some have come from our village and many others from our dis-

Farewell to Puschel

tant church congregation. Even more have come from various parts of Europe: from Sweden, Holland, and Bodenseehof, the Torchbearer Bible School in southern Germany. All have come because of Lydia, who never liked to stand in the spotlight. Most of the guests only knew her by the name of Puschel, and they knew she was only 28 years old when she died. At this farewell party, the question in the room, whether spoken or unspoken is, "God, why?" This question remains unanswered in the minds of those who loved her dearly.

Some bow their heads. Others stare at the coffin lost in thought. A few gaze at the picture of Puschel projected on the wall. In the picture, Puschel is looking happily in the distance as if she were looking God directly in the eyes, as if the two of them have something important to talk about.

Among those grieving are counts, barons, and journalists. Many of them accompanied Puschel over a period of several years both in friendship and in prayer. And, of course, Lydia's distant relatives of the big Holmer-clan are also in attendance.

As the pastor from Bülow, I greet the funeral guests. "We are not gathered here to put Lydia, our daughter, on a pedestal, but instead we are here because we want to praise God and thank Him for our Lydia." Lydia's Uncle Reinhard, from Elbingerode, talks about Jesus the Good Shepherd. "No one can snatch the sheep from the Father's hand. God gives us eternal life."

Lydia was rich; she didn't have much money, but God gave her everything she needed. She walked with Him as she endured the horrible disease that eventually took her life, and yet even as it affected her physical well-being, it never was able to touch her courage and her love for God and for others. This was evident because Puschel had friends all over the world, some of whom she knew simply because they belonged to the family of her Heavenly Father.

After the worship service, many come to the burial at the cemetery in Serrahn, 30 kilometers away. This is where Lydia's grandmother, who went before her into eternity, was buried in 1995. At that time, 12-year-old Lydia sat with us beside her *Oma's* deathbed.

After the interment, we gather together for coffee and cake as well as a time of praise and thanksgiving. Many tell stories of their experiences with Puschel. An old woman from our village describes how she always enjoyed it when Puschel came by to visit on her four-wheeler. Tabea, one of Puschel's cousins, says, "I knew Puschel before she became so wise. She was always ready to have fun ...." Some of her other cousins immediately agree. Friends from the Torchbearers and even some of the patients Puschel knew from her various stays in the hospital also share. At the end of this time, Puschel's foster sister expresses herself. She clears her throat – she's not used to speaking in front of so many people. "Puschel impressed me. For me, no one lived out their faith, love, and hope like Puschel. She always told me, 'I know that God's plan is perfect.'"

Let Us fix our Eyes on Jesus

Over a year has already passed since the funeral. After her 5-year battle with cancer, Lydia is finally home. Writing this book is very painful and yet at the same time very wonderful. While we pore through the journals Puschel wrote, we are continually surprised. We are learning about our daughter! For example, we discovered that from the very beginning of her illness, Puschel talked it over with God and discussed with Him what her future would hold. We learned that Puschel saw a common thread of God's presence and direction in her life. God lovingly wove in special experiences to prepare her for her final five years here on earth. She saw her time both in Sweden and El Salvador as pivotal in building a foundation for the last chapter of her life. She knew His hand was upon her, and she welcomed His loving presence. Puschel spoke to many young people in Germany, Sweden, and America, sharing with them how God was working. She also willingly shared with her friends in one of her blogs what God was revealing to her:

We are learning from our child, Puschel

> God does wonders. And this includes more than Him just keeping me here on this planet. One day I will die, like each one of us. And I am confident that I will enter a world more beautiful than I can ever imagine.

Puschel was, at her core, a grateful person. All who knew her saw this time and time again. God opened her eyes to a simple truth that is easily overlooked: the importance of thankfulness. She realized God gives us many opportunities and reasons in our day-to-day lives to thank Him. Where we live, what family we were born into, and which people we meet along the way are all minor details. We cannot change the influences of our past, whether positive or negative, or from our family or from our friends, but we do have a choice in how they mold us in the future. This is why gratitude was so important to her and why it became an integral part of her life.

I will experience a much more beautiful world

"I notice the everyday details of life and get excited over the little things," she said in a radio interview eight months before her

14

death. "I always knew it on an intellectual level, but now I have experienced what really is important in life. The most important thing is to keep my eyes fixed on my Heavenly Father. I noticed that the times I was down and out, and thought, 'Jesus, I can't do this anymore,' were times when I was concentrating on things other than Him. When I put my focus back on my Father, I was changed, and joy returned to my heart."[1] For this reason, the words on her gravestone read, "Let us fix our eyes on Jesus, the Author and Perfecter of our faith."[2]

We are fortunate to have a glimpse into Puschel's heart through her interviews, her journals, and her blog. Before Puschel set off for El Salvador in 2006, we created a website – *www.puschel.holmer.info* – so that she could regularly inform her friends about her work in Central America. She used this blog to share fun stories and keep everyone updated on how things were going in El Salvador. Later, this was also the best means of communication for both of us to keep in contact with her friends concerning the state of her health. At the same time, she continued to write in her journals her personal conversations with God. Not only did we borrow from these various communicative forms, but we also asked some of her friends to share from their experiences with Puschel. We wish more of her friends could have told their stories and we could have included more pictures, but we simply ran out of room. Puschel was a normal human being like you and me. Yet her normal included a deep passion for both God and people. This will become apparent as you read the following pages of her journals and letters. She certainly didn't write them for publication purposes, but we are certain she would be pleased with our sharing some excerpts with you.

---

[1] Taken from an interview with *ERF Medien,* broadcast on 05-11-2011 from the program "Colando."
[2] Hebrews 12:2

Puschel's Childhood

1982. We found ourselves in East Germany in the deepest time of the German Democratic Republic's (GDR) regime. So much was different then compared to what we consider normal today. I had just completed my first theological exam; I was studying to be a pastor. My time working as a vicar in the Mecklenburg State Church was almost over when I was completely surprised by being drafted into the military. It seemed more like a demonstration of GDR-power than a necessity. It should give all people a sense of not being able to count on anything or anyone. In the middle of my second theological exam, I had to quickly finish the written homework and shorten my term paper, because I was unexpectedly assigned to the Civil Service[3] division. I have to admit I was a bit angry with God at this point. What was all this about?

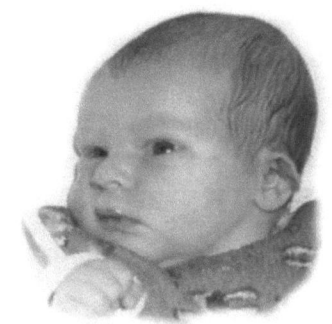

Baby Lydia with floppy ears (1983)

In May of 1983, my wife Eva-Maria was nearing the end of her pregnancy. Of course, I really wanted to be there for the birth, as I had been with our first child, Titus, but I was stationed more than 100 kilometers away, so it looked like it would be rather difficult to get there in time. However, I was determined to make it work. As the due date came closer, I waited expectantly for the news from the clinic in Wriezen saying that my wife was in labor with our second child, but I heard nothing. Days passed. The due date came and went. Then I got a call from home asking why I hadn't come for the birth. A little girl was born, our little baby Lydia. I learned that Eva-Maria had indeed sent me a message by telegram: "In labor!" However, it had not been passed on to me by my superiors. If I had

---

[3] At this time in Germany, men were conscripted to serve a minimum of one year with either the military or with the Civil Service. I wore a uniform which was different from the regular military, and built buildings and fences instead of being trained to use weapons.

received the message, I would have had a 3-day leave for the birth. The excitement over the birth of our healthy baby girl was overshadowed by my anger towards the carelessness of the GDR system. Infuriated, I wrote a letter of complaint to the General Secretary of the Socialist Unity Party of the GDR, Erich Honecker,[4] concerning the manner in which this was handled. Shortly thereafter, I received a response: I was given a whole week of leave! It was obvious God saw the injustice and straightened things out for my benefit. Now I was able to enjoy the little one and her mother at home much longer than previously planned.

After being stationed for less than a year in Jabel, near the towns of Waren and Müritz, my time with the Civil Service was over. It was then that we moved *Muschel-Puschel* to Bülow, on Lake Malchiner, to start my first congregation. The parish was located on a beautiful piece of land. The grounds included a picturesque view of the lake hemmed in by the surrounding wilderness of the northern shore. The expansive land of the church grounds looked untouched by human hands; so much of it remained unadulterated.

It was here in this small village of Bülow, population 70, that *She developed a mind of her own* Lydia grew up. She was an adorable little girl, and her pleasant personality was all a mother and father could wish for. At first glance, her fair blonde curls transformed her into a little ray of sunshine. Her way of life was cheery, sunny, and carefree.

It's the best with Mama

Our dear Lydia developed a mind of her own very quickly and demonstrated her own unique style. Because of this, people would joke at times about Lydia possibly being switched at birth. However, we knew without a doubt that Puschel was

---

[4] Erich Honecker was a Communist politician who ruled over the East German people from 1971 to 1989. Later he also took on the role of Head of State as Chairman of the State Council. He was key in organizing the construction of the Berlin Wall, as well as was responsible for ordering soldiers to shoot people trying to escape over the border.

ours, genes and all, and that she belonged in the "Holmer-Bülow Clan."

In the following years, two more siblings were born, Esther and Silas. Lydia wasn't fully aware that another little sister came right before Silas, but was stillborn. It didn't seem to upset her too much that Mama had had a really big belly for a long time, but came home from the hospital without another sibling.[5]

We did not dramatically show our sadness and loss to our children, and because they often bounce back from the harsh realities of life more quickly than adults, Puschel soon returned to the normal daily routine. Most of her time was spent with her older brother, Titus; both of them created their own games and roamed about all over the countryside together. Lydia could also quietly occupy herself for hours, whether in her room or outdoors. She was always busy "herum-muscheln."[6] One day when she was about five years old, some people came for a visit. Suddenly someone said, "And this is our Muschel-Puschel." This nickname, soon to be shortened to just "Puschel," became so accepted that many subsequent friends and acquaintances didn't even know her real name. Puschel loved to follow me everywhere when I'd work in the yard, and she always helped with whatever I was doing.

We had about 20 sheep at the time that were helpful "lawnmowers," since we had three hectares of land to take care of. Moreover, their wool was a valuable addition to our meager monthly income, as pastors in the GDR did not make much. To Puschel's great delight we had ducks swimming in the pond, bunnies cuddling in their hutch, and cats prowling through the weeds or dozing in the sun. "Muschel-

With Papa outside (1987)

---

[5] However, later her friend Eva told us that during her internship as a pediatric nurse, she really struggled with the death of her little sister.
[6] "Herum-muscheln" is difficult to translate. It means she was always busy creating, playing on her own, but also always involved with whatever was going on, ready to help and ready to have fun.

Puschel" invented all sorts of games to play with her animals and looked after the duck family. Sometimes she tried to train a little lamb or feed another with a bottle. One such lamb was named Fridolin. His mother died right after he was born, so Puschel begged to bottle-feed him. And feed him she did! Consequently, he followed her everywhere, even when she went shopping. Sometimes we found him in her room as she worked on her homework – they were inseparable.

One day Puschel came outside with me to "help" slaughter a duck. It was not abnormal for her to see an animal killed in order to have a delicious roast; death was just a part of life. She stayed by my side as I plucked feathers and finally pulled all the innards out. Little Puschel watched every step very closely and suddenly said, "Papa, may I?" So I watched, amused, as her short right arm disappeared into the duck – all the way up to her shoulder! It was no problem at all for Puschel to accomplish this task. This humorous scene is forever etched in my memory.

Puschel grew up in this idyllic village, similar to the "Noisy Village" that Astrid Lindgren often described in her books. Like in the stories, childish pranks often occurred. In the evenings, at the end of their daily adventures, the siblings discussed whether Mama and Papa needed to be told of their experiences. Puschel was often of the opinion that parents really didn't need to know everything. She often talked her older brother, Titus, whom she admired and looked up to, into various kinds of mischief. She herself had most of the fun ideas, but usually didn't have the strength to carry them out. One day, when Puschel was about seven, the village's recycled paper bin was set on fire. It burned for days. Rumor had it that it was the pastor's kids who were to blame. "Tante Holz,"[7] manager of the little grocery store, "Konsum", (a popular store during the GDR era), firmly protested, opposing anyone who was of that opinion. She sharply told them, "I will put my hand in fire to prove the innocence of these children – it was not them." Other children perhaps, but Puschel and Titus? Never! Years later, Puschel confessed that it really had been her brother who set that fire, initiated by herself. Only by this confession could "Tante Holz" believe that. Of course Puschel hadn't wanted it to burn so long, but it wasn't that big of a deal, at least not in Puschel's eyes. To her, life was always beautiful

---

[7] "Tante Holz": Tante = aunt, but it´s a German word to an older woman – friend of the family

– one shouldn't stress over such silly little things ….

In addition to her mischievousness, Puschel was a true artist. Starting at a young age, she enjoyed drawing and painting pictures on cards and letters for friends and relatives. This talent certainly did not come from her father but instead her mother, who is the artist of the family.

The Worst Times are Over

Puschel, along with her brother, Titus, experienced the harsh reality of the socialist GDR only for a short time. In September, 1989, Puschel started school.

Compared to brother Titus, her encounter with true socialism was not as severe. The previous year on his first day of school, Titus was separated from his class and made to stand alone on the playground while his peers were addressed as "the smarter ones" and were congratulated as they came forward, one by one, to receive their pioneer scarves.[8]

With big brother, Titus, and little sister, Esther (1987)

---

[8] "Die Freie Deutsche Jugend" or The Young Pioneers was a group created in 1946 by the former leader of Germany's Communist Party, Ernst Thälmann. It was similarly organized like the Scouts and the Hitler youth, but more focused on teaching socialistic ideologies to children ages 6-14. Each child that participated received a blue pioneer scarf to wear with their uniform for holidays, festivals, and special events. There were only a handful of families who did not allow their children to participate, and our family was one of those few. We made that decision because we did not want them to make oaths to the state, but to make their vows to God alone. The political system did not look favorably on those who opted out (even though membership was optional), and those families and children were

The strategy of the socialistic educational system was to make sure those of us "stick-in-the-muds" really knew and deeply felt that we were "standing on the wrong side." Everyone needed to see how very alone one was when one refused to move with the times. Thankfully, Titus's little sister, Puschel, had a very different first day of school. Change was in the air and we could feel it coming. A few weeks later, everything was drastically different.[9]

Now in school, Puschel proudly walked the three kilometers with her big brother to the neighboring village where their school was located. When the weather was good, they would ride their bikes down the narrow "KAP Street"[10] from Bülow to Schorssow. Sometimes they took the bus to and from school. However, when they needed to be at school earlier than the bus schedule allowed, they went by foot along the country roads. Often tractors driving by would pick them up and give them a ride. Once in a while Papa simply forgot to pick them up from school, but they were forgiving and knew he was always so busy.

My Papa – the Mayor

In 1992, I was voted into the position of mayor for several of the neighboring villages, because there were very few candidates who didn't have a past connection with the GDR regime.[11] It was the

Puschel's grandpa featured in the newspaper

first free election since the GDR fell. "My Papa is the mayor," declared Puschel proudly to whomever, whether they wanted to know or not. The times were changing, even for the pastor's kids.

In the days following my election, Puschel's grandfather made the headlines in well-known newspapers and magazines because he

---

often ostracized for their decision. This is one of the many ways the socialist government persecuted our family because of our faith.

[9] November 9, 1989, the Berlin Wall came down, and with it the GDR's Socialist regime.

[10] KAP or "Kooperative Abteilung Pflanzenproduktion" (Cooperative Department of Plant Production) which was more commonly called the LPG "Landwirtschaftlich Produktionsgenossenschaft" (Agricultural Production Guild). This street was mainly used by farmers driving their tractors back and forth between their fields and homes.

[11] Many people had worked under the Socialistic government so long that they knew nothing else. It had been their life, and they had simply followed what they were told. They had no idea how to live democratically, let alone lead others in the new democracy.

had opened his home for Erich Honecker's asylum.[12] In the eyes of the grandchildren, this was another reason to proudly look up to their grandfather. Of course, Grandpa, who was always loving and merciful to all, was simply Grandpa to them. In their eyes this wasn't out of the ordinary. Why shouldn't he help a man in need? They really didn't understand who Honecker was.

In the extended Holmer family, our children were four of over fifty grandchildren. Lydia saw this as a gift from God. Titus was the oldest boy of the Holmer clan's cousins, and Puschel was the first

The animals have to be cared for in the winter. The Holmer family baling hay

of all the girl cousins. I personally have nine siblings, and Eva-

---

[12] About a month before the Berlin Wall came down, Erich Honecker was forced to resign as General Secretary. His colleagues, along with his people, were infuriated with him, accusing him of high treason, embezzlement, and many other dishonest activities – many wanted him dead. Honecker was put under house arrest when he became very sick and was released to be treated. Because he no longer had a home and so many people were threatening his life, there was no safe place for him to live while he recovered from his month-long stay in the hospital. It was then that he sought assistance from the Evangelical Church in Berlin-Brandenburg, where Puschel's grandpa, Uwe Holmer, was a pastor. Uwe Holmer offered the Honeckers a home at his parsonage that was like a little village for the disabled. Many Christians were incensed that Pastor Holmer was helping the Honeckers because Erich and his regime had discriminated against them for so many years. For instance, while he was in office, he didn't allow Christians or their children to study at universities. Instead they were humiliated for their faith. Pastor Holmer's clear demonstration of forgiveness and reconciliation caused an uproar in the church. As Christians demonstrated against Pastor Uwe, this act of loving his persecutor drew the curiosity of the media.

Maria has four. Some of them have up to eight of their own children, so every family reunion was a large, but fun, affair. The older the cousins grew, the more colorful was our time together.

Starting in 1999, Grandpa Holmer, whom Puschel and all the grandchildren admired and loved, planned an annual "Vacation with the Grandkids." In the beginning, everyone came to Bülow each year, but when Puschel got sick, we started meeting in Serrahn, where Grandpa Holmer lived. All the grandchildren gathered together to learn about their grandpa's decades-old love for Jesus, and each one became a child of God.

Unfortunately, Puschel couldn't always be a part of the week-long "Vacation with the Grandkids." However, when she was available, she loved to see as many cousins as possible. It brought her joy to hear about Grandpa's beliefs and his wisdom in life, and during this time she always got to know her Heavenly Father better. Years later, when Puschel was so sick, even though she didn't like to speak in front of large audiences, she accepted Grandpa's request to share about her life with Jesus.

"Vacation with the Grandkids," (2005) – Grandpa Holmer loves to have all his loved ones with him

Ronja the Robber's Daughter

Puschel's cousins knew she wasn't an angel, but that she loved to play pranks. However, they still respected her and would attentively listen to her. Her cousins, Reinhild, Almuth, and Magdalena wrote: "Puschel was like Ronja the Robber's Daughter.[13] She was free, held her own when rough-housing with her brothers and male cousins, drove a Trabbi[14], and constantly made fun of us clueless `Big City Kids.´ (After all, we came from a town of 7,000 residents!). To us she was also like Pippi Longstocking[15] – strong, independent, the animals' best friend, and always filled with some sort of nonsense. We were like Pippi's friends, Tommy and Annika. She showed us how to break rules (of course without getting caught), to bale hay, and to ride a horse or a donkey – or see how interesting a crypt can be. Her ability to break an apple in two with one hand remained her secret, even though she tried to explain it many times. Not even all boys can do that …."

A Choice for Life

For Puschel, the church congregation was a part of her home. At the time she moved with us to Bülow, there was no congregation. In 1984 we found everything, the church building and the people's

Puschel as a schoolgirl (1991)

spirits, in ruins. Fifteen years prior was the last time they had a pastor, and the church board had long since dispersed. In the summer one of the four churches would hold a couple of services, but that was it. So when we arrived, everything had to be started anew and be rebuilt. Puschel, along with her siblings, was a part of this reconstruction. They brought their

---

[13] A character from one of Astrid Lindgren's stories
[14] Also known as a Trabant, a very common East German car
[15] Another one of Astrid Lindgren's characters

friends and classmates to church, which was how it all started. For Puschel, spiritually, her personal beliefs began to quietly grow. She never talked a lot about giving her life to Jesus at the age of nine. However, later in an interview she shared:

"When I was nine years old, I lay in my bed and gave my life to Jesus. I told Him, 'I have heard so much about You and it seems that You are pretty important. Because of this I want to know that my life belongs to You.' Over the years my request grew to be that I would live for Him one hundred percent. Along with this commitment, I also promised Him yet another thing: He could do whatever He wanted with my life …. He is doing just that." In her journal she wrote:

One can trust God! He directs and leads me often in wondrous and amazing ways! As a nine-year-old girl, I lay in my bed and trusted God. It is true that I am slowly realizing that one can never stop learning from God.

At the village school, Lydia was more like a gray mouse,[16] but afternoons at home she skipped happily through the yard, thought up her own games, painted and drew masterpieces, explored the peaceful village, and meandered through the meadows. After Reunification,[17] a family from West Germany relocated to our village, and Puschel began to learn about horses - not only how to ride, but also how to care for them. She often rode with these newly-found friends - Giesela and her two daughters, Konstanze and Lucia, who eventually became her best friends in the village. The long rides, the childish pranks, and the peaceful village setting really stabilized Puschel and gave her a great internal balance.

A strong love for horses began to grow in Puschel. While finishing high school, she completed an internship at a large horse-breeding ranch. After graduation, she was very sure of one thing: she wanted to work with animals. She applied for several positions that involved the care of horses, and then waited and hoped. But she only received letters of rejection. Suddenly, she was hit with the question, "What now?"

---

[16] The term "gray mouse" indicates that Puschel was an inconspicuous, unobtrusive, normal child at school – she blended in with the rest of the students and could easily go unnoticed.

[17] When the wall fell and people could again travel between and East and West Germany.

Aidlingen

Puschel during her time in Aidlingen

When Puschel's dream of working with horses and becoming a qualified horse groomer didn't work out, her grandfather approached her and asked: "What do you think about Aidlingen?" Aidlingen is located in southern Germany and is a home of deaconess "Sisters". One of their endeavors is helping young women find their professional calling. It is very important to Puschel's grandpa that his grandchildren "study something decent." He would love to see his eldest granddaughter well-trained and starting her own family. Making money and having a career, though good, aren't crucial. For him, the most important service to society and to children is the upbringing and education of children as well as a loving and supporting family. Going to college or university, from Grandpa's point of view, isn't bad. But often times young women then want to have a career - why else would they get a college degree?[18] In Grandpa's opinion, mothers who pursue a career don't make children a priority.

But it is not only Puschel's grandfather who suggests Aidlingen. We, as her parents, see the benefits of Aidlingen as well. It probably would be very beneficial for our 16-year-old country girl to meet a few young Christian people her own age. Plus the shelter of the deaconess "Mutterhaus" would be very helpful for her growth and independence. Of course, Puschel can choose herself what she would like to do with her life. Housekeeping does not really interest her. Her sense of tidiness is, politely put, not particularly strong. She would have to give up nature, her freedom, and her animals for a while. Nevertheless, everyone encourages her to go to Aidlingen.

---

[18] The system in Germany works differently. Students can finish school after 10th grade and do an apprenticeship, a three-year program to become trained in a certain field. Nurses, for instance, do not have to go to college in Germany. Carpentry, midwifery, occupational therapy, nursing, accounting, for instance, are all professions for which you do not have to attend college.

Besides, Tabsi, a good friend of hers from a neighboring church, wants to go with her. Puschel can only imagine herself gone for one year, doing an internship in housekeeping.

We cannot really tell how homesick she is during that year and how badly she must struggle to continue with the internship. The deaconesses are even less likely to understand how much the life-loving country girl from Bülow, who wanted to become a horse groomer, has to adjust to her new life in Aidlingen. But she wrestles her way through it and writes later about that time:

> *God led me to Aidlingen through my grandpa in 1999. That's where I really learned how to interact with other Christians. I am becoming independent. God gave me inner peace in all decisions. God also gave me loving parents who helped me wrestle through this time. I still see myself on the train, still in Mecklenburg, already overcome with homesickness. I thought about how wonderful it is to be at home here. This verse came to my mind then: "Do not be anxious about anything, but tell God what You need."[19] And that is what I did, because there are thousands of people in far worse positions than myself.*

Puschel makes the best of everything

Puschel makes the best of everything. That means she accepts things as they are and at the same time rejoices over what she has, as much as possible. So, even though she respects the strict rules of the deaconess "Mutterhaus"[20], she also enjoys her own freedom. Her friend, Tabsi, from Mecklenburg writes:

> *"One of our chores was to sing in the youth choir. During rehearsals we always tried to sit next to each other. You cannot really say that Puschel paid much attention.... During `super boring´ explanations, which were inevitable and part of the re-hearsals, she would just turn the music sheets and start drawing portraits of the two choir sisters, Annette and Christel. I couldn't believe my eyes when I watched her draw portraits or pictures like that. She could perfectly capture features and traits with simple pencil strokes. I had become friends with the two sisters quickly and showed them Puschel's portraits after choir. They*

---

[19] Analogous to Philippians 4:6
[20] Translated: "mother-house"

were so amazed by these drawings that Puschel was appointed to draw big backdrops for children's musicals."

Two girls from Mecklenburg in southern Germany, Tabsi and Puschel

Puschel really enjoys her time with the other girls. Some of them are from neighboring villages and thus enjoy a few privileges. When there is a youth night in Gärtringen, a town 7 kilometers away, Puschel doesn't think twice about going with everyone when she is asked, even though she is not allowed. And it's not just one, but many youth events. Through them she develops friendships with a group of young people around her age – yes, also boys (oh my goodness, and that's through the deaconess "Mutterhaus"!) who that shape Puschel's life.

At some point, we parents visit Puschel in Aidlingen. We experience the hospitality and kindness of the "Mutterhaus" and are grateful to see that our east German country girl is so well integrated in a faithful, Christ-centered community. One day, we are walking through the "Mutterhaus" when we come across Puschel working.

Her chore is cleaning a big, wide, marble staircase. However, everything is already clean, at least in Puschel's opinion. So, Puschel is standing on the stairs, holding on to the handrail, with a cloth underneath her feet which she wiggles a little back and forth, and smiles broadly at us. She is very excited to see us and explains, when we ask what she is doing: "Well, I'm cleaning, of course. I'm just doing it my way." In Aidlingen she also meets Myri, whose real name is Myriam. She is a little older than Puschel, and the two remain friends until the end of Puschel's life. Myri wrote some of the lyrics for the musicals that were performed by the children's and youth choirs in and around Aidlingen. For some of these musicals Puschel drew the backdrop. She does not take any of this for granted. Her friend Myri later writes about the time she first met Puschel and their early encounters:

When Puschel first came to southern Germany, she was very much shaped by her small world in Bülow. Everyone that met her heard about her dad and her mom, her animals, and the nature in Mecklenburg. Even then she was always happy to help, which led to her bringing up the person she inherited this passion from - her dad. Sometimes I thought to myself that every second sentence begins with "Papa...," "Mama...," or "Mecklenburg...." She simply was still the little country girl who loved her village and her family above all. And this was not going to ever change – except for the "little girl" part.

That, God changed in pretty much every way. In the beginning of our friendship, Puschel loved being part of activities and participating in everything. Later on she would lead and organize groups and initiate different things. I would have never dreamed of seeing Puschel talk in front of a big group of people, or seeing her write things for others to read. All of that she did years later – with only one goal in mind: challenge people to trust God more. Puschel wasn't a writer, an academic, or a big public speaker. Her heart simply belonged to and focused on God. She loved Him so much that she followed what was important to Him without compromise: people. This helped her do things she would have never thought herself ca-

With her friend, Myriam (2001)

pable of doing when she left Aidlingen as a 17-year-old. My first encounter with Puschel was actually indirect, through others. I only heard of "Puschel", and that she was an intern at the housekeeper´s house and could draw really well.

As we had just finished writing a musical, she drew a poster to advertise the upcoming performances. Underneath they had written: Drawings: Lydia Holmer. I remember thinking to

29

myself, "But this is a drawing by Puschel!?"

Puschel didn't like people taking away the fun of things, because fun was the most important thing.... For the longest time her favorite saying was, "God gave you a face. you have to smile on your own." Just as straightforward as possible – that's what Puschel liked best. Basically, nothing was ever a problem for her. And it was hard to make her realize that "boys´ clothes" didn't really look nice on girls, and that wearing a little bit of mascara wouldn't automatically transform her into a "fashion doll." At the end of her internship year, Puschel decides for herself to stay down south and start a nurse apprenticeship in one of the hospitals of the Aidlingen "Sisters".

However, after she turns in her application, she is told that she is lacking proper social behavior. That might have been the result of taking a bunch of special trips to the youth group in Gärtringen; one of the "Sisters" didn't like that at all.... Puschel's application is refused. But even though it is a big disappointment at first, it doesn't cause a crisis for her. She turns to the future. In her diary she writes:

...Slowly but surely the summer came around and everybody kept asking what I was going to do next. Myri had invited me to go for ice cream in Herrenberg. Suddenly we got a phone call from Sister Anne, whom I knew through Sister Christel.... She offered me work at the Korntaler orphanage for half a year, where she was the director. She also suggested I stop by the home for the aged. I did that and ended up working there from November until January/February.

During that time I was able to establish a friendship with Myri and to meet up with Lena and Co[21] occasionally as well. Sister Anne advised me to apply at the Olga Children's Hospital. I did that and was promptly invited to the selection process. Since I had never been to something like that, I got a little scared. But I asked God to calm my heart. In January I started feeling His peace. And during the whole selection process, I felt God's presence.

The entire time I thought to myself that this could be the next place for me, as the animals of Noah's ark were printed on the hospital letterhead.... And since Sister Christel, Myri, and I had just performed the musical, "Action Ark," with the

---

[21] Her housekeeping colleagues

children's choir, actors, and "Pro2,"[22] this seemed to me like a small hint.... The next day, while traveling home, I was standing in the cold at the Berlin central train station. I called my dad, who told me that I had gotten a call from Stuttgart. A verbal acceptance from Olga Hospital! That is guidance! This hospital is the biggest in Germany. It's supposed to be a good apprenticeship. The wait was totally worth it. Especially as I am experiencing life with God more and more – meaning my "cooperation" with God is getting better and better....

Happy Moments – Little Gifts from God

In between her time in Korntal and the start of her apprenticeship in Stuttgart, Puschel gets to spend a few weeks at home. She enjoys that a lot because, even though she has made a lot of new friends in southern Germany, her home is and always will be Mecklenburg.

...It snowed heavily last night. Lucia and Konstanze came home late from school. So, I took Saba for a ride through the snow-covered countryside. Just the two of us – it was incredibly beautiful. Later I went for a walk with Joshi [the donkey]. Suddenly, I saw Lucia coming home from school. We ran toward each other and started throwing snow at one another.... I am so happy about the little things in times of independence like these. Why can't our eyes see these things more often?

February 28th, 2001 – I am very excited to see what God has prepared for my life. I often realize that God does things we couldn't even have dreamed of. Such a life is so exciting! Our youth group meeting never took this long before. It was a lot of fun. We studied a small part of the life of Jeremiah. It must have been hard for Jeremiah when God told him that he was not allowed to get married and have a family. But I know that God's ways are good, even if they are different from what we want or imagine or dream of. God also changes the importance of material things with us. Never would I have thought that I'd move

---

[22] A small girl's choir from Aidlingen

into a city for three years. But God prepared me for this time. And He did so in such a sensitive and gentle way that I didn't even notice. Let's see what else God has planned with my life. I imagine, briefly summarized, that I will do my apprenticeship as a pediatric nurse, work for a few years, start a family with five kids, and then help in the church community... but deep down I already know that it will never be this way. One can only be amazed and wonder!!! And never forget to trust in the Lord...!

Did God already put a hunch into her heart of what was to come? A hunch that He would one day ask something of her that we would all be afraid of?

March 19th, 2001 – "I am just a guest born in this world!" This saying just came to my mind. I think it has a special impact. Does it mean that we should take care of this world because it isn't ours? That my real home is somewhere else? We talk to people about our home on earth but never mention our real home! Do we behave like guests? I mean, we are supposed to feel at home but don't we sometimes settle down a bit too much on earth? Lord, let me be a blessing to the people of this world! Help me to also talk about my "other home"! I know You help me and will carry me through it all – happiness and sorrow. Thank you!

A Completely Different Sister

"Hello world, here I am"

Late in the summer of 2001, Puschel starts her apprenticeship at the Olga Hospital in Stuttgart. She loves working with children. In the different hospital units, in school and in the dorms, she meets the other students. Most of them don't care much about a personal relationship with Jesus. This is generally not really a big deal for Puschel, as she grew up knowing many people who didn't know Jesus. She likes people who question her and her faith, is grateful for every challenge, and at the same time she lives her faith as consistently as possible. She builds friendships we often don't even know about. One particularly good friend from her apprenticeship time is Eva, who loves horses just as much as Puschel does. Eva thinks back to this time:

Puschel caught my attention right away during our introduction round in our seminar group. She was one of the youngest in our class, which was pretty quickly very apparent. And she spoke proper German. She couldn't always understand everything when we spoke "southern" German. She'd then always say: Could you please repeat that in a way I can understand it as well?

She talked a lot about her home, about Mecklenburg, and her parents. And after only a few minutes, everyone knew that her dad was a pastor and that she loved the outdoors - one of the things that linked us together right away. Our first conversations were about horses and everything regarding them - not about our apprenticeship. One day during class we were talking about death, and neither one of us was comfortable talking about it. Puschel told us that her mother had a miscarriage once. Later, a younger sister died during delivery. This had affected her deeply. After that lesson, Puschel and I went for a walk together for the first time and she told me about Jesus. I had a million questions regarding life after that. Was this the reason why

Puschel was so much more relaxed and at ease than I was most of the time? A whole lot of deep and important conversations followed before I decided to give my life to Jesus one year later. Puschel and her friend Myri played a vital role in this decision. Puschel gave me a small Bible with an inscription. This Bible has accompanied me through life ever since. I vividly remember the moment of her handing me this Bible. It was like a "holy moment." She made it a celebration. Typically, you wouldn't have expected something like that.... However, collectively these moments were the starting point of a much more exciting and thrilling life with God.

Puschel's Foster Sister

The Holmer family in 2003 with foster daughter K.

During her apprenticeship, Puschel met K., a girl whose real name we won't use for her own safety. We, the parents, met K. through Tanja, our children's ministry staff leader. Tanja had led the children's ministry for a church in southern Germany before she came to work in our church. Soon after she had settled in Mecklenburg and had become acquainted with the church, the the phone in her office rang. It was K. calling from an office of child protective services in southern Germany. K. is seventeen, originally from Turkey, and a Kurd. She has been living in Germany since early childhood. Describing her life would fill a book of its own: rejection, being left behind, violence - all of which she experienced as a child. For years she has more or less been living on the street. When she was a little girl, she went to Tanja's classes at church. Now, almost 10 years later, she is seeking help. When children's protective services pick her up off the streets, she suddenly remembers how much she loved those children's church classes with Tanja. Child protective services are clueless what to do, and K. doesn't know where to go. She mentions Tanja's name to them, and they arrange the phone call. K., of course, has no idea where Bülow is or how tiny it is. But she asks, "Tanja, can I come visit you for a few days?" And Tanja agrees. At this point she does not know what she agreed to, because all the horrible experiences during K.'s childhood have led to identity and personality problems. For us in Bülow, a lot of new experiences soon lay ahead.

K. attends our Sunday church service together with Tanja, but the proximity to God is too much for her. She wants to pray with Tanja but can't. In the past she has come in contact with Satanism and other demonic practices; these weigh her down like a heavy burden and are also physically noticeable, especially during prayers or church services. Even though K. wants to open herself to God, she seems like someone who is remotely-controlled; she balks, and even responds aggressively. Consequently, we are all tested in our faith. These fights we have to put up with are very intense and hard for all of us. But they are also healing experiences because K. comes to know God's power and love and we witness it in her. Puschel hears about all of this from afar via phone. After a few weeks, the child protective services arrange for K. to start psychotherapy and addiction therapy at a mental health clinic near Stuttgart. We ask Puschel to visit K. every so often. So Puschel starts caring for K. together with her friend Myri, with whom she is spending a lot of time these days. We try to help as much as possible from afar. But for K., this therapy is extremely hard. During this time, child protective services asks us to become K.'s foster parents for the few months until she turns 18. K. herself asked for this. We eventually agree to it. Shortly thereafter we get another phone call from child protective services. "K. ran away," the guardian says. "If we can't find her, we don't know what is going to happen." What now?

Two days later the police find K. and take her to a locked acute psychiatric unit. We have to probe for a long time - since we aren't K.'s official foster parents yet - to find out where she was taken. We finally learn that she was taken to the

A Turkish Kurd becomes Puschel's sister

psychiatric acute unit at Olga Hospital, where Puschel is currently doing her apprenticeship. For Puschel and Myri this is clearly a miracle from God. It becomes a lot easier for Puschel and Myri to visit K. now, and they do this as often as they can. Every so often, K. is even allowed to leave the unit by herself. She then uses that time to visit Puschel in her small and rather chaotic dorm room, where many girls from her study group feel at home. Puschel, Myri, and K. talk, pray, laugh, and cry a lot together. During those days, K. gets to know God and she learns to pray. She gradually starts to build trust in people and in God. "Puschel, Myri now, and then again Eva shaped me," K. tells us one day. "For the first time in my life, I met people who took of me – not for any particular reason, but just because, but just because I was important to them." And later Puschel is home when K. is baptized in "Malchiner See" at home in Bülow. K. stays almost three years with us in Bülow. This is how a Turkish Kurd became Puschel's sister.

Isn't That Amazing?

During her apprenticeship, Puschel works in a cancer unit for children. Every day Puschel faces the little patients and their desperate parents who are confronted with all the questions that death prompts. Eva remembers this time together:

Puschel drew and painted a lot in her small dorm room and gave these pictures away to a lot of the girls in her course. She lived her faith in Jesus on a daily basis without being intrusive or admonitory. She didn't judge anyone, which was so impressive to me.

She had so much love for everyone around her that she seemed to overflow with it – and you could feel that it ultimately was God's love.

At the end of that chapter of her life, Puschel wrote in her journal (August 2001):

Isn't it amazing how much I am able to do? It is not meant to sound boastful but to be praise to God. I would have never thought that I am brave or strong enough to go to Aidlingen. I would have never thought I would be allowed to paint the backdrops for the musical, "Action Ark," let alone that I COULD. We often think too negatively. God simply gave me the chance to discover this.

I have been given amazing abilities by God, which He has

only partly shown me until this year. Where do I, for instance, get the strength for gratitude and joy in order to be a role model for what a real life with Christ looks like? But I am still not radiating enough gratitude, if you ask me.

I am not sure if it is a character trait or if we can learn it. I think joy about other people transfers easily to others. You just have to show them the joy. "It is like a mustard seed, which is the smallest of all seeds on earth. Yet when planted, it grows and becomes the largest of all garden plants, with such big branches that the birds can perch in its shade." Mark 4:31-32.

Sweden

An Adventurous Start
to an Adventurous Time

Puschel's desire to be closer to God brings her to the decision to take a few months off after she finished with her apprenticeship and before she starts working as a pediatric nurse.

Grandpa Holmer's advice is to start working as a nurse for now, because work experience and starting a family would be a bit more tangible. Years later Puschel tells her grandpa: "Grandpa, I am so grateful for everything. And your advice was always great and wise. But to this day I am so glad, that I didn't take your advice this one time...."

Puschel and her friend, Eva

There is a youth center of the Torchbearers, a Christian youth organization, in Holsbybrunn, (Småland) Sweden. Here Puschel and Myri would like to work for the upcoming three months. Myri has to cancel her plans last minute. So Eva decides quickly to jump in instead and join Puschel. Even though Puschel is now a lot more independent, she is still very happy to have Eva tagging along, for alone it is never as much fun! The adventure begins. Eva writes about her memories:

We happily met at the Stuttgart central train station to start our journey to Sweden about one month after our final exams. Off we go to Frankfurt, from where our plane to Sweden was supposed to leave! We got to Frankfurt with a ton of luggage and the sense of being well-prepared - only to realize quickly that our flight to Sweden wasn't actually really leaving from Frankfurt but from Frankfurt-Hahn. That's an airport for cheap airlines and about 80 km (roughly 50 miles) outside of Frankfurt. But time was running out and our airplane wasn't going to

38

wait for us. This left us scraping together a big chunk of our money to take a cab, because taking the train would have been pointless. We made it to Frankfurt-Hahn last minute and were happy that, in the end, everything worked out. But this was supposed to be an adventure!

We were at the check-in counter and you wouldn't believe that despite all the hustle and bustle, the lady at the check-in realized that Puschel's ID had expired and was no longer valid. Without a valid ID, however, there are no flights to another country…. And thus we went, pretty depressed and with all of our luggage, to the bus station instead of onto an airplane….

There we sat on top of our bags and weren't sure if our journey had already ended or what we should do now. But both of us were wired in such a way that the inevitable didn't just throw us off the track so easily. For Puschel, problems really only existed to be solved anyway….

We suddenly remembered that we had already talked to Puschel's dad on the phone in Stuttgart. After sending a quick prayer to heaven, we decided it would be best to call home again. Perhaps it was somehow possible for Puschel's dad (who was mayor, after all, and knew many "important" people) to apply for a temporary ID in "cloak-and-dagger" fashion. In that case, we would go home to Bülow and leave from there, taking the old "Polo" and the ferry to Sweden.

And this is exactly what happened next. When we finally made it to Sweden, completely exhausted, we were greeted in a very warm and friendly way by the staff – in English. We didn't understand a thing at first. It turned out to be an advantage to have come by car, however, because everyone on staff was able to borrow the Polo to run errands. Puschel especially had no problem with sharing an insignificant "everyday object" like a car with everyone!

Vitality

Eva and Puschel adjust quickly to life with all these pleasant (and sometimes surely rather unpleasant) adolescents from all over the world. Puschel has a lot of fun with the "Amis"[23] in particular, so much so that (almost) everyone likes her. She likes to be challenged, especially athletically and preferably by the boys, as she can effortlessly keep up with most of them in strength and athleticism.

She doesn't particularly like to show her growth in faith outwardly. She continues to enjoy talking for hours with the others in the evening, jogging through the forest in the morning, laughing at funny things people say over meals, and going climbing with friends on the weekend. All the while, inwardly, she is growing closer and closer to Jesus, whom she consciously puts in the center

This kind of climbing is more like going for a walk with Puschel. She climbs "against" her little sister, Esther.

of her life - above all else. Thus, bit by bit, the external things become ever less important to her. That doesn't mean that suddenly she has no more joy in living life within "worldly things." For her there is no funny thing that can't be made even funnier with a little "Puschel pizzazz."

A somewhat older colleague – Harry, from Latvia, who works every year for a few weeks in Holsby – recalls an incident from this time:

In autumn, Puschel helped on our clean-up crew to rake up the fallen leaves. I quickly realized that something was up. She always had incredible fun playing jokes. One time she suddenly asked me if she could leave for 10 minutes, and I said, "Okay!" Of course, I figured that she was planning something, so I watched her and another girl as they sneaked over to the boys'

---

[23] German nickname for Americans

dorm, examined the fire escape, climbed it, and disappeared into the building. That was it ! A few days later, Brad (the cook) brought a small pail with frozen water into the dining room and turned it upside down. Out came an ice block – with twenty-some frozen toothbrushes in it. How we laughed – even though the boys didn't find it quite so funny, at least at that moment.

During our visit in Holsby we get a sense of how rooted Puschel is in the "Holsby family." She's glad, for example, when in the winter we come with our chainsaws to help remove debris from the wind damage. Or when we bring some youth from our congregation to visit in Holsby.

One day she is asked to help out in the kitchen. Although she never really learned how to cook, the chef sometimes lets her single-handedly cook lunch for seventy people. One day, beans are on the menu for lunch, which is always noon. Puschel puts the pot of beans on the hot stove about 90 minutes ahead of time. When the assistant cook walks into the kitchen about half an hour later, she asks: "What? You just started to cook the beans?" Startled, Puschel says: "Yeah. Why? We have plenty of time until noon."

Jesus, increase the heat of the fire

"Beans take about three to four hours!" Baffled, Puschel stands in front of the pot and asks herself how she is to get these beans done by twelve o'clock for lunch. There is no alternative. So she prays: "Jesus, increase the heat of the fire." When another staff member enters the kitchen shortly before noon to take the lunch into the lunch room, Puschel asks him to try the beans first. He tries, nods appreciatively, and says: "They are done. We are going to serve these now." Later we are often astonished by how many people around her were impressed by Puschel. Kirsten, a "special ed" teacher from Colorado Springs, USA, recounted some of her experiences for us:

I met Puschel in August of 2004 when I returned to Holsbybrunn, Sweden to work on staff at the Torchbearer Bible School that coming school year. We lived in Solhult, the house for single ladies, right next door to each other. She had come as summer staff but had decided to stay longer.

She was mainly the caretaker of our friend Amy, and I was the assistant to the principal, being involved with the students both academically and socially. Over the school year, Puschel

41

and I became very dear friends. She was quiet at first, but I soon discovered it was because she was still learning to speak English. Having studied foreign languages myself, I marveled at how quickly she picked up the language without all kinds of grammar courses. She wasn't afraid to try or to make mistakes, which helped her learn much more quickly. It was evident from the start that she loved Jesus with all her heart. I frequently saw her go off with her Bible in hand to spend time with her Savior. Whenever issues came up in the staff house, she would point us back to Christ – I knew she talked with Him all the time.

Puschel was a burst of sunshine in my life on a regular basis. She knew how to encourage me and cheer me up. I loved spending time with her, not only because her craziness was intriguing, but mainly because she loved Jesus with all of her heart. Everyone knew that Jesus was her Lord and Savior....

Help for Amy

Eva recollects about the summer:

We stuck to the Americans (Puschel thought they were way more cool anyway), which ultimately led to the rapid improvement of our English. We even had our devotions in English pretty soon. We were part of a really fun girls' dorm room where we really behaved like girls.... ☺ *Of course there were boys that Puschel liked, but that never was a real issue for her. One morning, Ric, who was the director, came up to us and told us that one of our co-workers had to be taken to the ER last night because of some psychological issue. He asked us to back the decision as a team. However, we weren't quite sure how to do that. So we started praying intensely for Amy.[24] Only a few days later, she came back to campus. Our leaders asked who was willing to share a room with her and would be able to look out for her. Puschel said that she knew this psychological disorder a little since she used to have a foster sister with similar symptoms. And so both of us ended up in Amy's room....*

Puschel becomes Amy's caregiver. At this point, she is the only one who has a vague idea of how to deal with a disorder like that.

---

[24] Name was changed

During the following weeks, Puschel calls home a lot, asks questions, discusses with us what needs to be done next, and we pray together. Amy's disorder comes from deep personality problems that have psychological and therapeutic considerations. And even though Puschel has experienced something similar with her foster sister already, she often reaches her limits within the next few months.

Puschel with Amy in Sweden

The Tool, Not the Worker

In the fall of 2004, Puschel writes in her journal:

It is about time to write down some of the things I have experienced with Jesus during the last few weeks here in Sweden. I am increasingly allowed to witness how important it is to be rooted in Him, to trust in Him, and to keep telling Him my thoughts throughout the day. I am infinitely grateful that I am His child and allowed to "play on His team." "This poor man called, and the Lord heard him; He saved him out of all his troubles" (Psalm 34:6). God often leads us differently than we would like. But He always leads us well. He has the foresight, not me! In Sweden, I was taken in with love into the community of Christ. Therefore, it didn't really matter if I understood them (language-wise) or not. They would always repeat things with patience if I sometimes didn't understand anything. Fairly early on I heard about Amy (I'm giving her a pseudonym). She was in a hospital for a few days because she didn't want to live anymore. When she came back, she wasn't allowed to be by herself because it would have endangered her life. But in the big team which was surrounding her with love, she was safe. God taught me so much through K., my foster sister. I had first-hand knowledge that nobody else on campus had. When I was told that I was going to work with Amy, I wasn't sure what that meant for me. We prayed a lot. Often Eva and I prayed together, just the two of us, as we often didn't understand the prayers by the Americans. We had to learn to cast our worries onto Jesus. He is the conqueror! He let me experience that He doesn't fail to hear every single prayer. I was able to experience how He wanted me here to encourage people.

The staff team fully supports Puschel. Yet there are many situations she needs to manage and pray through on her own. She writes about this much later to the director of the Torchbearers in Holsby, John Poysti:

Dear John - I told you about the verse that came to my mind when I thought about you all and your situation. "The Lord Almighty is with us; the God of Jacob is our fortress" (Psalm 46:11). Did you know that Martin Luther would take an extra hour to be with God if he knew he had a very stressful day ahead? I remember a time in Holsby. I went running. I ran through the area until I stopped suddenly with tears in my eyes. It was night and it was raining. There were sooo many problems with Amy and I just didn't know how to keep moving along. I was full of questions and told God that I had reached my limit. Suddenly it hit me: I had started to attempt solving all these problems on my own and out of my own strength. God showed me that the only way out of this situation was surrendering my worry, doubt, and fear to Him. For He promised to take care of everything. And you know what? He did it! Some of the problems disappeared right away, some didn't (and some of which I thought needed to be solved, didn't really need to be). The big difference now was that He had taken control again. I was only a tool, not the worker. I had switched positions without knowing it.
The result was that I realized I couldn't do it out of my own power and strength. I gave it all back to Jesus and let Him take

*care of things. I couldn't possibly be able to take responsibility
for a 30-year-old lady who had such immense problems that she
was thinking about ending her own life. In the eyes of some people, I was able to do that, but they simply didn't understand. The
only thing I could do, and had to do, was live through and in His
power.*

Despite her big responsibilities, Puschel has a lot of fun and always tries to let everyone else be part of it. Eva writes:

*Puschel often went running with the boys because she could
actually keep up. She was admired for that, which she liked even
if she never openly said so. Even when we went climbing, she
kept up with the boys, who were really impressed (the girls were
always impressed by her athleticism anyway). Puschel had – oh,
what a coincidence – many admirers. But the one she would
have liked the attention from was not one of them, what with one
thing or another. So she had to reject some of those boys. One
day we were called because one boy had hurt himself. It was a
wound on his leg, which I didn't think was that bad, but Puschel
took her time providing professional and extensive care. If you
asked me, she checked it a few times too often. How lovely for
him. It wasn't rare that we experienced gorgeous sunrises and
sunsets together. We celebrated small and big festivals. And
even the church services and devotions were "celebrations of
joy." No surprise at all that the summer was over way too
quickly, especially for me. I had to leave to go back home,
whereas Puschel stayed to take care of Amy.*

So Puschel stays in Sweden, while Eva returns home. Puschel's
English has improved enough to manage everyday life without a
problem. After a few months, her brother, Titus, joins her on staff
in Holsby for a few weeks, and later her friend, Myri as well.
Puschel's main assignment is looking after Amy. In that work, she
experiences moments of miracles and joy but also often moments
that take her to the edge of her limits. There are wonderful moments
that help Puschel mature spiritually and personally as well.

Gratitude and Faith

In between all the difficulties and joyful moments, Puschel finds time and peace to reflect in gratitude on everything she has experienced:

Holsbybrunn, November 22nd, 2004 – Father, my whole life shall be lived in worship and gratitude. I want to thank You all of my life. No matter what situations I face, I want to thank You. I have no right to complain about things. Who am I to complain? Teach me to recognize Your deeds, down to the smallest. I want people around me to see You within me. I want them to see the love, grace, mercy, and everything else You have for every single one of us in abundance. I want them to see who You are; yes, that nothing is too hard for You!

The more I realize who You are, the more awe and respect I have. At the same time, You bring me ever closer because You are love. Little by little I learn how to trust You more. My SELF doubts You sometimes, but my WILL to trust You is there. You are truthful to the core. And Your word in the Bible is genuine. Thank you for giving me the Bible. I am allowed to read it openly without being persecuted. I can study it. Why don't I spend more time doing that? Thank you for the time I am allowed to be here in Holsby. It starts with the houses and the country. You made it perfectly. The summers are gorgeous and the winters cozy. It makes me so happy to go for walks through Your nature. Thank you for my legs. Thank you that I am healthy. Thank you for giving me so much joy in athletics and for giving me the freedom to exercise here. Some people may think it is hard for me to work here. But I am so grateful for the surroundings I am able to have here. Lord, I want to give You thanks for creating me and putting me right here. You put me into a family that loves You and me; a family who taught me that You are the head of the family. You gave me a dad who is like me and to whom I can easily talk; someone who is smart, whom I can ask for advice, and who serves You; a dad who loves nature and animals and still likes technology; a dad through whom I have an idea what it means to be carried. He comes to visit me in faraway places and is genuinely interested in what I do. I was able to learn that money is not the most important thing in life. Lord, I want to thank You for my dad and that I have one in the first place.

And then You gave me this wonderful mama. She is con-

The Holmer family – Bülow early in 2005.

cerned for every one of us. She is a faithful wife and home-keeper. Without her, Dad would not be able to work. She loves to do our laundry for us. ☺ We have so much fun together, es-pecially when we are on vacation. At those times she still is this very young girl, not a grownup, who thinks about the next prank to play. I am the same way when I am relaxed. I know that Mom and Dad love me, even if they don't always have time for me. So who cares if they send me things, but no letter? It does not mat-ter. Their story of how they got married is a role model for my life. Dad asked her if she could imagine beginning a friendship that would lead to marriage and becoming the wife of a pastor in Mecklenburg.

Father thank You for my dad, being a pastor in Mecklenburg. Thank you for letting me grow up there, directly on the lake, with lots of space, and with animals I was able to take care of by myself as I got older. I have great memories of my childhood and almost no bad ones.

Titus: I am so grateful for him! You gave me an older brother, and that is so cool! He has a good heart. I think his is often much bigger than mine. He helped me become the person I am today. We spent a lot of time together. God, thank you that You have sent him to Holsby for a while. It is so special to see how close we still are.

And then there is "Mousy."[25] She sees what I need before I realize that I need something at all, especially at the table. She loves children above all. She has got the same sweet spirit my mom has and is learning to manage her life. She always thinks about others, not herself, and she does that well. Furthermore, she stands firm in Jesus. Thank You, Lord, that You taught me

---

[25] Esther's nickname

so much through Mousy and that she is my sister!

Now Silas, the youngest of us, who is growing up so fast.... I can have so much fun with him. He is shy when he doesn't know people. In addition to that, he is very athletic and technically gifted. Regarding school and learning, I think he doesn't care much, just like Titus and I don't. He has a smart head and a big heart for children. I can laugh myself to tears with him. Thank you, God!

Then there is K. - she came into our family a bit later. Through her, I think all of us got to know God better. Furthermore, she was my preparation for Sweden.

Thank you, Lord, for continuously being present in my life. You have changed the shy girl I used to be. You brought me to Aidlingen, where I was taught to be with other girls. That is where I met Myri, and You rooted me there in a special way. I learned that other families can become some sort of home!

Thank you for the time in Korntal that I could share with Myri. I was able to become more and more independent there. You taught me the beauty of caring for children and the elderly. It was an educational and good time. Thank you for helping me see that You have a plan for my life. During that time, Myri became a closer and closer friend to me. She is the pure opposite of my temperament, which often is a good thing. The children's choir and the school benefit from her personality. And when we do things together, we balance each other out. She has an incredible singing voice. During her studies, she had to study a lot less than many of the other students, I think, and she still did well. Thank You for the many things, people, and places we were able to get to know and experience together.

I am not sure what You have in store for me in the future. But I want to give You thanks because I know that You will take care of her and of me! Thank You for letting us go to Foehr[26] together.

During my three years in Stuttgart, You also put the families of Gaertringen into my life, especially the Baders and Zinsers, who are very important to me. They were my foster families during that time. Thank you for every single one of them! Father, I can see Your hand in my life continuously. Thank you!

---

[26] Small island in the North Sea

A Baptism in American English

One day the phone in Bülow rings. It is Puschel. That is not often the case because she has become very independent and doesn't talk much about what she experiences. This time she has a concrete question for me as a pastor: "Dad, what do you think? Lindsay wants to be baptized. She realized during Bible school and during her trip home this summer that being a Christian doesn't just include faith but also the baptism as a confirmation. So she asked me if I would baptize her. What do you think? Can I do that? Or will it cause problems?" I had never been asked such a question before, so I had to think about it quietly. Philip, who baptized the Ethiopian (Acts 8:26-40), was not an ordained pastor either. He was not even able to go through baptism lessons himself. The crucial part was acknowledging Christ.

So I told my daughter during our next phone call: "Yes, I am convinced that you can baptize her. Take your Bible and re-read the passages where it talks about baptism. Normally only ordained pastors or priests baptize in Germany. But there shouldn't be a problem for an American, especially since she is going to join a interdenominational church at home anyway." Shortly after, a small group of young people – mostly Americans – gathers in the forests of Sweden for Lindsay's baptism. For her, it is absolutely okay that Puschel from Germany conducts the baptism. Puschel does mention it again later, but she isn't someone who would talk about it at great length. Lindsay, the baptized girl, remembers that day and writes:

It was at the end of the summer in 2005 when I had come back to start the new school year. Puschel picked me up in Vetlanda, and I told her right away that I wanted her to baptize me. But I remember that when I initially asked her, she said, "What!? No! I can't baptize you!" And I know I said something like, "OF COURSE YOU CAN!" I remember thinking - why does it have to be only a "pastor" or someone "ordained." That's not truth. That's what man had turned baptism into. So I explained all that to Puschel and talked her into it because I had specifically wanted her to do it. We were SUPER close and I just loved how she JUST LOVED JESUS - above and beyond, simply and purely. She just saw Christ; she just saw her Father in everything, in every way, and would not compromise. She could neglect anything else except HIM, and it was beautiful - a single-minded pursuit of Him, wholly available! I wanted the baptism to be intimate, and even though I had wanted a bunch of the staff to witness it and share in it, I did not want a big show or party. So I invited those closest - our little circle of staff who knew each other well and had been there longer. I remember it was so cute because the boys came all dressed up in slacks and ties ☺, and we drove the van to the lake. I remember Puschel read two scriptures. One was Romans 6:8-10, and we sang a song or two. It wasn't extravagant or drawn out. It was just what I wanted...simple, intimate, and JUST JESUS! And then she submerged me in the water and out I came - a new creation in Christ! And then we played in the water and had a great time. It was very sweet and special, and I will always hold that time dear to me – not just that day but those couple years I had with her and everyone. We were very dear to each other. We got to spend a couple of years together, and we had some very special times and memories during that time. Puschel is one of my favorite people – ever - hands down. What I loved most about her was her unmoving, unwavering love for her Father, and the simplicity of her life that showed it. Thank you, Abba!

Ready to Leave?

Here I am in Sweden. It was supposed to be a time during which I was supposed to follow You and do something for You. However, You sort of reversed things and made it a time for myself. There is no other time in my life during which I've learned so much from You like I did during the past six months.

Thank you for sending Amy here during this year. Thank you that I am allowed to be here and witness Your miracles and see who You are! How clearly did I see that I cannot do anything through my own strength, and that my life turns upside down if I do not fix my eyes on You, Lord. How vital is and has been my morning quiet time with You, Lord! Father, my life belongs to You. Please show me if You are ever not my first priority. I don't have the right to keep my life to myself!

Thank you for all these friends from all over the world. Thank you for the times I was able to sit in on lectures, and that I can buy the CD's for cheap! Yesterday I took a nap and was thinking of the children in Stuttgart during the "Octoberfest." I realized how much more passionate I am for children who don't have real parents. I always think about the Philippians when I think about missions. I asked God at night if He wanted me to go there. I opened my Bible to Ephesians 4:17: "The word of God is a sword...." That brought my thoughts to Matthew 28:19-20: "Therefore, go and make disciples of all nations...."

Every so often, we participate in youth retreats in Sweden with our church youth. Puschel is especially happy when she gets to introduce "her young people" to everyone else. During one of those visits, we leave an edition of the magazine, *IdeaSpektrum,* on the table.[27] A few days later, Puschel is sitting at the kitchen table, looking through the magazine. Since she doesn't enjoy reading too much, she just looks at the pictures. A picture of an orphanage in El Salvador catches her eye: La Casa de mi Padre.[28] She looks at the picture and suddenly knows that there is something God is asking of her. But what is there to give? She doesn't have money, which means she can't support them financially. The only other possibility is to go there and help. The subject of missions has been occupying her mind for a while anyway. At this point she has no clue where El Salvador is. "Do You really want me to go there?" she asks God. "First off, I have no money. Secondly, I don't speak any Spanish either!"

February 7th, 2005 – I am just a small help and You can do those things without me. But You want to use me. Thank You! I can see how You bring Your work together piece by piece. You are a puzzle maker. I listened to the CD: "Your Word is a Light to My Path." Yes, Lord, I want to live in Your light! You are the meaning of my life. My light, my stronghold, my fortress...!

I am not sure where You want to use me. But here I am. And if it should come to an end here on earth, those around me shall know that I have only been a guest here on earth. To be with You in eternity will be the best part of my life! I cannot even begin to

---

[27] That's how Puschel recollects and describes it during an interview with Dominique Pfeiffer for the youth week in Gaertringen in 2010 (Video 4). http://www.youtube.com/watch?v=wGsm68FLy7o (Viewed on July 1st, 2013).

[28] English: The House of My Father

imagine. Wow, it goes beyond my imagination!

February 20th, 2005 – If You open the doors to El Salvador, I will go. If not, please give me patience to wait until You show me the right time and place. I am not entitled to wishes, but You know where my strongholds are and where I still need schooling. I just want to know You even better and love You even more.

February 22nd, 2005 – Lord, teach me to accept people the way they are and not to judge them for their actions. I want to learn to accept everyone through Your love. I want to draw people's attention to You, but I don't want to scare them away through my words. Still, I want to be bold. When I look at someone, I want to smile at him or her with Your love! Help me to do that with every person.

Thank you, Lord, for this morning with You. I totally slipped into questioning what's coming next in my life. There were a lot of worries. When I opened Your book again, You directed my attention to Matthew 6:24-34. Then I asked You whether You wanted me to take charge. I thought that I should start working in a hospital somewhere.

Puschel takes her Bible again and re-reads Matthew 6:33-34: "But seek first His kingdom and His righteousness, and all these things will be given to You as well. Therefore do not worry about tomorrow, for tomorrow will worry about itself. Each day has enough trouble of its own." That means she shouldn't worry. But is this supposed to mean she should not worry about where to go next or just not worry about provision for her needs once she is in El Salvador? She turns the page to Matthew 9:36 and reads: "When He saw the crowds, He had compassion on them, because they were harassed and helpless, like sheep without a shepherd." Children who didn't know who to ask for help.... Puschel is sure that God used this verse to talk to her. She decides to contact the orphanage in El Salvador and ask if they needed any help. About half an hour later, she shows this verse to her friend and realizes that the verse doesn't talk about "children" but of "crowds" or "people." This reading error, however, helped Puschel to make a decision.

I sent an email to El Salvador together with Hanna. If I am allowed to go there in Your name, Father, then please help Mom and Myri to understand that, too. Please prepare them! Lord, if it is not a good idea, then help me to be patient and wait for Your ways. Otherwise, I will be grateful and happy that You granted me this exciting adventure, haha....

M. yelled at me intensely about some dirty dishes. She even got very personal. Lord, I ask You for better companionship here at "Solhult."[29] Show me where I need to improve, but also please protect M. from heart attacks if she gets too upset with us. I forgive her for those things because You showed me the truth through Kirsten. Thank you for the friendships here!

March 8th, 2005 – We had our last family group meeting. It was a precious night. We told each other what we value about the other person as an encouragement! We are so differently made and individually valuable, Father. I often don't take enough interest in the people around me. And the people who don't know You are far too seldom on my heart.... It is a strange feeling to know that I will never see those people here on earth again. But it is YOU who connects us forever. Lord, only You can keep any of them from leaving Your flock. Father, teach me to approach people! Thank you, Father, for the prayer walks I was able to have together with Amelie. Thank you for blessing me through her in many ways. Continue to bless her life.

One of Puschel's best friends at this time is Alana, a young Canadian girl, who writes about Puschel:

My last memories of Puschel in Holsby: It was spring and almost everybody knows that this is a bittersweet time in Holsby. Spring is in the air, flowers start blooming, and a scent of summer is in the air, but most students and staff members pack their bags to go home. It was my turn now to leave Holsby. It was a tradition for everyone to gather in front of the main building and say goodbye. We did so on this day, too. I remember the big circle of my Holsby family. It was heartbreaking. I went around saying goodbye to everyone. When I reached Puschel, we both cried. I cannot remember ever seeing Puschel cry in Holsby, but on this day we cried together. When I said my goodbyes to some other people, Puschel had suddenly disappeared. I had no idea

---

[29] The single staff girls´ dorm in Holsby

where she went, but I figured that saying goodbye was simply too hard. I loaded up the car, and I waved to everyone as we slowly drove off. The street leading from campus to the main street is about 1km long. As we approached the main street, I noticed a girl sprinting next to our car. It was Puschel who, had run through the forest. She had picked a bouquet of wild flowers and was now handing it to me as a final goodbye. She was still crying. Her hair was tangled, as it often was. We promised each other to see each other again.... This is how I will always remember Puschel. Running. Wild. Happy. And always a sense of humor.

July 6th, 2005 – Alana left two days ago. There is a hole. Thank you for this friendship! Please help me not to neglect her, but instead let our friendship deepen. I am so tired of the goodbyes. At the same time I am excited to see what God has in store for this summer. Show me what's next, Father! Change me into someone who is more sensitive and more respectful for other people. You are the reason I am here. Your plans for our lives are so much better than we could ever imagine. I can fully trust You. This summer was packed with retreats, visits, and travels to Germany. Lord, thank you for Lissi, Inge, and Amelie, with whom I can always pray. Lord, show me my purpose in Holsby now, and let El Salvador answer. Bless the work, the children, and the staff there. Thank you! My deal with the Lord regarding whether I should stay here or not was that if He gave me a free sleeping bag, I will stay! One week later Eva calls me and tells me she is going to send me a sleeping bag.... So, I am staying until the end of October because I don't feel like I am supposed to leave yet. Lord, kick me out of the nest if it is supposed to be. Mid-September would be okay then. Lord, if it is meant to be, let this friendship [with Dan] deepen and help us to stay in touch beyond Holsby. He will be here this summer. Thank you!

Old Friends Go –
New Friends Come

September 14th, 2005 – This month was very busy again. Many friends left. But I was allowed to form new friendships, too. I could spontaneously go on a three-day canoe tour. In the beginning of this summer, Tom came. On that very day we talked about canoeing. I couldn't believe that something actually came of it. In the beginning of September, so only a few days ago, I could even go camping together with Jen, Dan, and Tom in Gränna. It was sooo good. Once we had to change our sleeping location because there were daddy longlegs all over the place. I have never seen that many in one spot. So instead, we stayed in a beautiful barn that night. The following day, we drove to Stockholm and spent the night in a forest.

Afterwards, we took Tom to the airport. Strangely enough, I still miss him. I hope we will stay in touch. Two days ago, I called El Salvador and learned that they could use my help starting in March. I am excited. Without God, without You, Lord, I cannot make a difference there. It is too big for me. Thank you that I finally know. Bless the remaining time in Holsby. Grant me wisdom for the planning for El Salvador.

September 10th, 2005 – I went for a walk with God in the forest this morning. I realized that I am to stay here until Christmas. I don't know why. I have a real answer from El Salvador now. Lord, thank you for revealing Your love and guidance to me over and over again. I don't have to raise funds. Thank You! I don't have to fear anything as long as I live through You. Thank You! One Wednesday after worship service, I got restless, grabbed my bike, and rode down the road to Wally and Donna. I asked God: "What are You trying to tell me?" And God said: "I love You." I was able to experience a bit more of His love.

Puschel is in Sweden for more than 18 months, which is a lot longer than she had originally planned. But the new direction is clear to her: She is going to El Salvador! One of the most important friendships for Puschel is with Wally and Donna. They were there when the Torchbearers started their work in Sweden about 40 years ago. They have become something like Puschel's surrogate parents. Donna writes later:

"Puschel came to work on summer staff that year, but when her time was about to conclude, she volunteered to stay on another year so she could give care to a needy individual. This is where I began to witness who Puschel really was! Her role was not easy, but she never complained. Her role went beyond the

normal hours, but she exuded unending faithfulness."

During that year, we were often together and shared a lot of precious fellowship. We were sad to see her depart Holsby, and yet excited for her future as she anticipated serving at an orphanage in El Salvador.

Puschel writes about her time in Holsby:

Looking back, I can only see the blessing in this time. Psalm 34:6 [NIV]: "This poor man called, and the Lord heard him; He saved him out of all his troubles." God confirmed these words for me every day anew in Holsby. The most important thing is to keep your eyes on the Lord, and the rest He will handle. Such certainty! I am so grateful to be His child. A child of the King of Kings! We should be grateful and make use of this privilege (which is available to everyone)!

Departure to El Salvador

Trust is Everything

Puschel's American friend Kirsten writes:
"I felt a little skeptical about her idea to go to El Salvador and asked her if she knew Spanish in order to work with the orphans there. She nonchalantly shrugged her shoulders `no,' and said she wasn't worried about the language – she'd learn it when she got there. Nothing was ever insurmountable for her. She trusted God to take care of all the details. What an example she was to me - her faith in her Heavenly Father made me examine my own."

Some friends suggest to Puschel that she join a missionary society so she would be safe-guarded better in El Salvador. But for Puschel that would take too much time, because it would involve missionary training and language classes. So instead, she told Gary Powell in El Salvador that she would be there as soon as possible. In her calculation, this means early spring of 2006.

Before she leaves, she keeps an important appointment back home: Her older brother, Titus, is getting married. After the wedding, however, she will immediately start her journey.

She enjoys her time at home until her departure. Over and over again she is asked, "How are you going to get the money for El Salvador?" Puschel answers: "If God wants me to go there, He surely will find a way for me to get there." As her parents, we think to ourselves if she is that certain, it will probably work out. And if God does not want it, He will prevent it. There are a lot of different suggestions about how Puschel could finance this trip, until someone finally suggests talking to the German social services department. However, surely Puschel cannot claim unemployment pay, because she went straight to Sweden after her apprenticeship and has never really worked in Germany.

Nevertheless, she approaches social services to at least file for unemployment. The office worker only says, "We will check your application and get back to you." Just a few days later she gets a letter from social services: she will get unemployment pay – and a lot more than she would have even thought. The calculation is based on her salary during her apprenticeship. Thus, she is able to save up money for three to four months. She never spends much on herself anyway. In the end she is able to save up enough for a round trip ticket to El Salvador as well as a trip to see her girl friends, Alana in Canada and Liesl in Idaho. She is able to meet friends as well before she goes to Central America. While she is still at home, she writes in her journal:

> *February 2nd, 2006 – It has been a while. A lot has happened. I have been back home for about a month already. God, You often show Your love for me through other people. I want to share Your love with others.*
> *Now quite some time has passed. Lord, thank you again for the time in Holsby. Thank you for all the people I got to know there. Help me to always long more for knowing You better and seeing You more. Help me to set aside enough quiet time with You. I don't want to stand in the way of You transforming me into the woman You want me to be. Thank you for Your faithfulness. I can always count on You. Thank you for my family. Thank you for this place of my childhood and for letting me grow up here in peace. Arouse all of Mecklenburg! God is writing a story with us!*

It's Possible Because of Modern Technology

Before Puschel takes off, we establish an internet website through which she can update her friends all over the world.

Here she portrays her first impressions on her way to El Salvador via a few stops in the USA and Canada:

> *February 2006 – I've got my flight tickets to El Salvador in my hand. As you can see, God has provided everything I needed so far. In fact, I can even say five words in Spanish*

fluently already: "Hola, Me llamo es Puschel."[30] And, "Gracias!" I want to trust my Lord with all my heart. I certainly don't know what to expect. I am excited for the country, the people, just the place God has for me. What a big God we have. Praise the Lord!

March 7th, 2006 – Dear friends, thank you for your prayers. The journey [to Canada] was smooth. I am with Alana in Calgary for the next couple of weeks....

March 25th, 2006 – I had a good flight. My time with Alana was awesome. I didn't meet any bears or mountain lions.... I am in Idaho with Liesl and her family now (she has five siblings). We have a lot of fun together. I was also able to visit Tom's family and meet up with Russell (friends from Sweden – if any of you know them). Oh, and we went skiing on the "Schweizer" without breaking any bones. I will be on my way to El Salvador the 27th and 28th. I thank you all so much for all the prayers and support!

---

[30] Hello, my name is Puschel.

A Different World

Culture Shock

The founder of the La Casa de mi Padre orphanage, Gary Powell, manages one of the Hilton hotels and lives in San Salvador with his family. Gary saw the neglected children in the streets and wanted to give them a new perspective. So he founded the orphanage. Because of his full-time job at the Hilton, he has many good contacts with people, even up to the government circle. The author of the article in *IdeaSpektrum*,[31] Thorsten Alsleben, heard about Gary's work through his wife, Rocio, who had once worked for the Hilton Hotel that Gary managed.

March 28th, 2006 – I am in El Salvador now! Father, You made this world so wonderfully for us. A new chapter of my life is starting now. It was 37 degrees[32] when I landed here. The country is beautiful. There are so many different kinds of trees and birds. I am blessed with my own room and bathroom. I can see a beautiful sunset from my window, a window that faces the garden/backyard. My day is winding down. Thank you, Father, for my life! "You are the light of the world. A city on the hill can't be hidden" (Matthew 5,14 [NIRV]). Lord, I am here for You. Never let me forget that! Be my strength. I want to know more of You.

Central America is a new world for Puschel. She doesn't speak Spanish and she did not go through a culture training class. She simply observes and is amazed. But she never doubts that it was the right decision to come here. In her personal journal she writes:

March 29th, 2006 – Father, this world is so different. I live in one world here, but really it is two. I met the children for the first time today. This place is a big challenge for me - too big. But Lord, this was Your plan, so You have to lead it now. I realized through the conversations I had today that I am the only

---

[31] Issue 4/2005
[32] 98.6 Fahrenheit

nurse here for 50 children. At first I was shocked, but then I prayed. Shortly after that a woman approached me who will be helping me for a little while. She explained to me that she has information for diseases, specifically for El Salvador. She always hoped that it would help someone someday. Thank you for bringing her here this week. I don't understand any Spanish. But I love the children. It is normal to always have a child on your lap. A little boy talked with me today for about 10 minutes, and I did not understand a word. These children are poor, yet even they are wealthier than so many others in this country.

Yes, and there is the other world: I have a beautiful big room here. The towels got changed on the first day already. I don't think I'll ever have to clean my room. I went to Gary's hotel today[33]. It is a completely different world. People are amazed and think I am crazy for spending a night at the airport before I came here. Nobody here understands that I can't afford a hotel whenever I please. They also cannot understand that I have never seen more than Germany, Sweden, Denmark, and Italy, and that I haven't even been to Egypt. I was offered water, and when I finished it, a new one came right up. Crazy. I probably attracted a lot of attention in my shorts and sandals. I attract attention anyway, because everyone has dark hair here. Even the little boys were totally excited because of my blond hair and blue eyes. Lord, I don't want to turn any heads here but serve You alone and be a light. Oh, and then there is the thing about not being allowed to go anywhere by myself.[34] Help me not to be bothered too much by this. Since I love going for walks with You, this rule seems rather hard. Father, bless this room and turn it into a room for me to "go on walks with You." Your will be done, Lord. Right now I hear gun shots in the neighborhood. That's another thing. There are a lot of houses with armed guards standing in front of them. The orphanage has a guard, too. Father, thank you for staying the same, even though my whole world is changing. You are my rock and I do not want to trust in anything else. People call me brave for coming here. Thank you that I do not have to be brave, (and I don't feel brave either), but I am only doing Your will. Thank you for being my Father. Help

---

[33] The hotel Gary runs; it's his full-time job.
[34] For safety reasons. El Salvador is a country with one of the highest crime rates in the world.

me to always be "me," whether I am in the orphanage or at the hotel. I now ask You for a deep and restful night.

March 30th, 2006 – A new day has grown old. Rolando is my chauffeur. It takes us about 30 minutes to get to the orphanage. We see a lot of decayed houses; people stand by the streets to sell things, wash cars, beg, or sell flowers. Everyone parks wherever they want to. Sometimes a car is parked in the middle of the intersection. People honk a lot. Noise from everywhere, heat, exhaust fumes, diesel-air, dirty streets, no traffic regulations, a lot of pick-up trucks, overflowing busses and a lot of trees.... People sitting on the side of the street. People walking to work. People in the middle of the street.... Father, bless El Salvador! Bring joy into their hearts – that is You! I have been given a lot of duties. God, I cannot do any of them. Lord, grant me wisdom. You know what I need to do because You made everything. Thank you for the Powell family.

March 31st, 2006 – Another day has passed. Again, I have gotten new information about my work here. God, I need You at my work every minute. Remind me to always stay close to You while I am working, because You know exactly what needs to be done. There was rain and a big thunderstorm tonight, even though it wasn't supposed to start raining until May. Thank you for sending the nurse my way. Your timing is just always perfect.

We went to Pizza Hut with the family today. And we went out for ice cream. They told me that I have to start practicing my driving on Sundays. The streets are crazy, but You will be with me...! LORD I do not want to get lost here...! Thank You, Father, for the laughing children's faces and for those who are just learning to laugh. I can see You laugh through them! Allow me to always be happy seeing those faces and help me to never overlook it in my everyday life.

Puschel always talks enthusiastically about everything whenever we get to talk on the phone or Skype with her. She updates her friends through her website. "Don't worry if You don't hear from me that much. I am fine!" But she has to learn to adjust to the peculiarities and mentality of the people now:

April 9th, 2006 – Father, help me. I never want to say

something about people which would hurt them if they heard it. Father, do You think I should start a Spanish women's Bible study? Lord, show me! Help me to learn Spanish and help me to know You better. Make me realize every moment of my life what You did for me, a person worth nothing by myself but through You made very valuable. Lord, to You be the glory. Help me to embody and radiate the hope I have in You to others.

Lessons in Brushing Teeth

Puschel is supposed to update the medical care at La Casa de mi Padre to a level that can be a model for Central America. Initially this means focusing on the simple things: daily hygiene for the children. They need to learn to brush their teeth and wash themselves on a daily basis. When the orphanage opened, there was nobody for this job. Puschel feels that the most important thing is for the children to learn how to take care of themselves. And that is not limited to hygiene and the children.

The native nannies have to change a few of their lifestyle habits as well. Of course, there is room for tension and friction. Puschel rubs them the wrong way when she tries to enforce certain new things. All of that occupies her mind inwardly, for she wants to demonstrate the love of her Heavenly Father to those people.

March 18th, 2006 – Father, You entrust me with things that You know challenge me. Even though we make a lot of mistakes, You do not take those responsibilities away from us. Lord, help me to focus on You during our time in the morning. Allow it to become more fervent. Never let me forget that I am only a stranger, visitor, ambassador, wanderer, traveler, foreigner. I have a home with You! This earth is not my home. I am made for something much bigger. I will never be completely satisfied on earth because I am made for eternity. A lot of Christians have a very hard life here until the very end, and yet they know that the end is only the beginning of an unbelievable new life. This is why God puts incomprehensible milestones in our path sometimes.

Puschel and some of her "kids"

Gary Powell started this work with an unambiguous example: George Mueller, the "Orphans´ Father of Bristol" (England). George Mueller had made it a rule never to ask for money. When a woman asked him what he needed right now, he apparently answered: "Your Heavenly Father knows your needs" (Matthew 6:32). This is how Gary and his team do things. Together they ask God, not people, for everything they need.

April 26th, 2006 – Father, I have to laugh thinking about our visit at the doctor's office. Six children and five adults in a normal car. Lord, keep watch over our children and open our eyes for mistakes we might make, so that none of our children will be harmed. I'm thinking of Salvador who had been given twice the dose of his [anti-]convulsion medication for a while before the nannies discovered they made a mistake. You know that we only have money for these children until about May 10th. Father, You have taken care of them so far. I trust that You will also do that this month. So I ask You to give these children what they need. (This prayer got answered with a $15,000 donation!)

Puschel only gets enough for her basic needs: food, accommodation, and a little spending money. But when it becomes apparent in the summer that La Casa must give away Teki, a beautiful big dog, because the money for food and such is needed for the children, Puschel "adopts" him and uses her spending money to pay for the dog's food. Puschel knows that peaceful Teki is a wonderful "therapy dog" for the kids. So Puschel sends a message home that says, "We have a new family member. His name is Teki Holmer."

May 19th, 2006 – Father, Your existence is not measured in time. You have a different "time." I also don't want to depend on time. I always want my life to depend on You. All of my "plans" I give to You, so You can show me what needs to be done next and where I need (or am allowed) to go next. I don't want to hold back anything from You. Lord, thank you for Your grace, for allowing me to serve and know You.

If You want me to stay here longer than just one year, I do not want to stand in the way of that any longer. Lord, I don't deserve to work with such qualified, good, and faithful people. My life is so rich with You, Father. Time flies by here. I have already been here two months. I feel at home even though my Spanish is rather limited. I can't imagine not knowing this country or these people anymore. Whitney[35] came May 9th. Lord, thank you that she is here and that we get along so well.

Growing Love

Slowly but surely, Puschel grows into her work and gets to know the culture better. Her love for the children also grows and grows steadily.

May 22nd, 2006 – Father, I never want to judge or gossip about people. Help me to stand up and say NO when other people do it. Thank you – and no thanks will ever be enough – but thank you, nevertheless, that You gave Your life for me. It is my desire to lay down my life for my brothers and sisters and share Your love. Let people see Your love, how You love me unconditionally. Help me to be honest and sincere with You and the

---

[35] Gary's oldest daughter

people around me.

May 29th, 2006 – Thank you for last Friday, when we took 15 children (ages 3-7) to the dentist. Father, I love these kids more every day. Thank you for the joy You give me with them. Father, please show me clearly when to go to Germany. Fall or spring? Or at a different time? And then encourage me to come back here. Help me to learn Spanish quickly... and to accept the fact that I cannot speak it yet, and that this, too, is part of Your plan. I love You. I cannot connect it to something specific, but Father, I love You so much. Help me to stay in conversation with You throughout the day. Father, a lot of times I complain to other people or worry about things instead of coming to You and talking it through with You first. Father, teach me to change that.

Puschel tells or writes to us about happy, everyday life – and sometimes about her general worries. For instance, it is important for her to get her visa extended so she doesn't have to go to one of the neighboring countries and come back again first in order to spend another three months in El Salvador. She wants to officially work and stay at the orphanage for one year. The work with the kids and also with the team is getting better and better.

Everyday Life in El Salvador

June 22nd, 2006 – Salvador had a little girl as his "bed neighbor." She is only one year old and looks very malnourished. The papers on her bed state that she has a heart condition. I took her out of bed when I heard that she rarely has visitors. I was allowed to feed her. Then a small, rather poor looking man approached and told me that he was her father.

He was very grateful that I had taken care of her. He took her into his arms and stayed the entire afternoon. On the day she was discharged, I saw him once again. It touched my heart deeply when I saw this man walk home with his daughter in his arms. A man who doesn't have much materially, yet with so much more love for his daughter than many rich men would give. I saw a bundle of love walking home. In this world where they shoot each other out of hatred, there is a father who gives his daughter everything he can give without any wealth - that is, love! And ... my visa got extended! Thank You, Father!

Puschel soon has a very heartfelt friendship with all of the Powells, especially Whitney, the oldest daughter. She lives with them and enjoys that more and more. Being away in a foreign country without any family relationships would have made her work and life there a whole lot harder.

July 21st, 2006 – *Father, there has been so much going on. You have shown me so much - Trust. Father, that's the example I want to set for the people of El Salvador. It makes me so sad to see that nobody trusts the next person. That means that they cannot trust You either. Lord, I do not know how, but I want to set an example for them in this while I am here. It is my prayer that they will learn to trust. Help me to see every person from Your point of view and love them. Thank you for the patience You give me every day. Our team is not really a team yet, but I can see Your hand at work. Help me to do the right thing so I bring You closer to them. Thank you so much for Whitney. I can only marvel at what You have done with our living in one room together over the past three months. Thank you for her!*

July 24th, 2006 – *Whitney and I had a little accident on July 21st. We fell. She has got a headache, and I have to wear a neck brace. I lost half of 3 teeth in the front and hurt my chin and lips. On the next day, Saturday, we were able to see a dentist who was on call, and thus I got my teeth back. The only thing is, the two front ones are still displaced. Father, please don't let there be any more complications. Thank you, Father, that nothing more happened.*

As it happens, Puschel got hurt as she was trying to prevent Whitney's fall. Unfortunately she herself fell, hit her chin on the curbside, and broke off 3 of her front teeth. Since Puschel has good insurance for El Salvador, she can visit the best doctors.[36]

---

[36] Much later, when Puschel has been home for a while and needs to go to the dentist for a different problem, the dentist is impressed and confirms that the colleagues in El Salvador did an excellent job.

A close friendship forms between Puschel and Whitney.

Whitney writes:

Puschel was not in El Salvador very long, just over a year, but in the time that she was there, Puschel managed to touch many lives. She was a true example of Christ's love to the children of El Salvador, daily living it out. Most of my memories of Puschel are of her with the children at La Casa de Mi Padre (La Casa). Every day we would make the drive through town together to get to La Casa. This trip was always full of adventure, as the streets of San Salvador are crawling with crazy drivers and people running across the street right in front of you. We had several near accidents. One time on our way, Puschel looked at me and said, "Whit, I don't have my driver's license with me." I told her to just drive carefully since we were halfway there. Just two minutes later someone suddenly stopped in front of us and we hit them from behind. We laughed for a long time after having to explain to the police that it was our car and that we were driving it legally. But in that moment it was rather scary.

Once we arrived at La Casa, our first stop everyday was always the "baby room." That was the room where all the children under two years of age lived. The walls were lined with cribs so that there was space in the middle for them to play and not get hurt by the bigger children running around outside. As soon as Puschel walked into the room, the little ones had their arms up ready for her to hug and play with them, as did all of the children at La Casa. Puschel loved playing with those little ones, and so did I. Every day while the older ones were at school, we would take these precious little ones out into the main area to play. Puschel was always coming up with new games to play with them. And I would always turn up the music and get them dancing. But probably my favorite thing we did with them was to play leap frog. This consisted of Puschel and me taking turns running and jumping over the children. They would laugh so hard when we would land on the other side. When we were not playing games with the little ones, we would spend hours just holding them and letting them know they were loved. I remember Puschel holding little Ana Julia and telling her that she loved her, but that

Jesus loved her more. You could always see His love reflected in her eyes when she would do this.

Puschel also helped get dentist and doctor appointments and answered calls all the time on how to help a sick child. During the time that she was here, a local university offered to give all the children free dental care. So every Friday afternoon, Puschel and I would take about 15 children to this university for them to have their teeth cleaned and cavities filled. The hard part was that it was just Puschel and I to watch them for hours. We created some pretty crazy things to keep them entertained while they waited for their turn in the dentist's chair. Anything and everything became a toy, from hairnets to gloves. One time, Puschel took one of the children's sweatshirts and wrapped it around his head. Then she asked him what he thought he looked like. He smiled from ear to ear and said, "I am a grandmother." We could not stop laughing at his answer.

One of the little ones Puschel became very attached to had epilepsy. During her time here, he had several seizures. Some of them were so bad that he had to go to the hospital. On one of these occasions, we spent the whole day at the hospital with him, to give his caregiver some much needed rest. While we were sitting beside his bed, watching him sleep, Puschel just kept stroking his face and telling him that he was loved very much. As soon as the doctors came, she started asking them so many questions. I had a hard time trying to keep up translating all of them. Puschel loved him very much and even tried to convince her parents to adopt this sweet little boy.

Apart from working at La Casa de Mi Padre together, Puschel lived with our family. It was so much fun having someone in our house that spoke a new language. Puschel taught us little phrases in German all the time. Some of them would get us into trouble, but they were always fun things to say like "squirrel" or "little matchbox." Carlos was the most interested in learning new phrases. He even made up a few of his own, which always made us laugh. It was also fun to paint and draw together. But my favorite thing was to stay up late at night talking and getting to know each other more.

Puschel always wanted to cheer everyone up. She always had a positive outlook on life, even in the hard times. And what inspired me the most was her devotion to God. I remember her always getting up early to read her Bible and spend time praying before she started her day. That was something that struck me about her. She always put God first and eagerly desired a relationship with Him. Puschel also had a sincere heart and genuinely cared about others.

Puschel always wants to be aware of her identity. She is a child of God, a "princess" of the King of Kings and she wants to live like that, too.

August 7th, 2006 – My Father, don't let me forget the foundation of our relationship. I am Your child, the child of the King. You set me free and promise to keep Your word. Father, keep my faith simple. I want to trust like a child. I don't want to get tangled in big theology or instructions.

I want to consistently see the purpose of my life and my status before You. Who I am. I am Your child. You love me (indescribably). I am Your representative, and on my journey I can invite as many people as possible to the "festival of life." I want to represent You with clarity and truth. I want to pass on Your love and not worry, for You are the one with whom it all began with – the Alpha and Omega!

September 4th, 2006 – My Father, I want to be a woman who belongs to You with all of her heart. Heal the parts which keep me from serving You with my whole life, heart, and vitality. Thank you for the new house we have received for the children. Lord, I thank you for last week, for those hard but instructional days.

It doesn't get easier as the year winds down. In the fall, Puschel wonders more and more whether she should stay longer than a year in El Salvador or not. Everyday life, however, moves on and Puschel enjoys her "family," her "sisters," her "little brother," Carlos, and her Father in heaven:

October 15th, 2006 – It is Sunday. Carlos is sitting with us at the table and is reading his children's Bible. Father, let this little boy grow up knowing You and living in Your love. Let him follow You all of his life. Thank you for Your words, Father. In view of 1 Peter 2:4-6: Father, forgive me when I only love my life and do not think of other people, and when I am not sad thinking about those who are lost. I do not deserve to be saved; they do not "deserve" to be lost. I also want to learn to ask and expect everything of You, to be consistent in You. You see all those people I meet. Open their eyes and help them see. Lord, I ask You to bless this day and let it be another adventurous day with You. I want to see You!

By now Puschel is fully integrated into the team of La Casa. Repeatedly, they experience financial shortages. However, the staff doesn't write fundraising proposals but talks to God about their needs. Puschel also does that, and it seems to bring her joy:

Oh Father, we repeatedly get to points of running out of money. We have nothing left now. But I still know that You will take care of these children. Father, bless the man who could maybe help us financially. Lord, if he doesn't belong to You yet, open his eyes and heart to see the wealth he could gain in knowing You (Ephesians 1:18). We drove to the office with the girls today. One of them was used as a prostitute in the past. Heal her, Father! Take away the problems between the boys.

A Man By the Side?

The question of friendship and love, marriage and family is on Puschel's mind also. Puschel is not a person who talks about these things with anybody, not even her closest friends. But she does write about it in her journal:

October 9th, 2006 – ...and if one day a man asks me to be his wife, it shall only be a man who follows and loves You with all of his heart. Lord, let me be hungry to study and embrace Your Word. A huge example for me in this is Brother Yun: "The Heavenly Man."[37] I want to love You more and more.

Thank You for Carlos' small and happy personality. Let him grow up in Your love and the desire to serve You with his life. I also want to thank you for T. Lord, You know our friendship.

---

[37] Puschel recommends this book about his life ("The Heavenly Man: A Remarkable Story of Chinese Christian Brother Yun") to all of her friends.

(Whoops, wasn't it his birthday...?) Please show me clearly what You want this friendship to be. Thank you for his personality. Thank You for his love for people and You. Thank You for saving him, for his smiles, his respectfulness, his adventurousness... I could go on. Father, in everything I want to thank You for the things he has taught me. I want to ask You to bless him and help him grow in love and trust in You - this new year of his life. He is Yours! Thank you! Father, You are incredible in bringing people together and letting friendships form and grow. How did we deserve that? It's incredible how meticulously You know and have planned everything, even before I was born! I can only be amazed! This is a day You have made. Help me to be happy and enjoy this day.

November 12th, 2006 – *After I told him happy birthday a month ago, I want to thank you once again for T. today. Father, I ask You to form him into a man who honors and pleases You. Let him grow in his faith and trust in You.*

December 30th, 2006 – *Thank you that I finally have gotten an answer regarding him (T.). You have someone much more suitable for me, Father; it shall be someone I am friends with for the rest of my life. My best friend. You know it.... I want to adjust my life to You anew. I want to see people as You see them.*

Later on Puschel observes that God had known what was to come, which is why He left the answer to the question of partnership open. One last journal entry regarding this topic was written a few years later:

August 31st, 2009 – *I can only be disappointed by my life if I do not set everything, my whole life, before You, Jesus. My Savior, give me strength and courage to consistently rely on You. I am tired of being disappointed. Jesus, I want to focus on You. Much too often I was hoping for a boyfriend and the opportunity to get to know him better. And then they left again. And if there happened to be a man with character, he also had a girlfriend on his side. Anyway, if there should ever be a man who fell for me, it would be a miracle (there are still miracles today) since I am not "normal." On the other hand, what do I want with a guy who only likes me because I am outwardly "normal"? The reality looks like that. But Jesus, I know that first of all, there are miracles with You. Secondly, I am not sure whether I will still live here in a year. If not, it would only be one more person mourning. And anyway, I don't even know if it is Your will. Jesus, please just help me to enjoy and be happy with the things I have, instead of mourning or longing for the things I don't have or wish for. I want to have a joyful heart simply because You are YOU. And my most heartfelt prayer is that people may see You through my life.*

There is Something Brewing...

Gradually, something is coming at her of which we aren't at all aware. Something is brewing in secret over her – and, therefore, over us: a tumor is growing in Puschel's right pelvis. At home, we don't notice that she has become tired. But then once during a Skype, call she casually mentions that she has pain in her pelvis and her right leg. She doesn't mention, however, that she can barely sleep anymore and has trouble sitting, too.

Whitney is Fighting for her Life

Meanwhile, another serious event gains center stage at Christmas time. Whitney, the oldest girl of the Powell family, gets into a terrible car accident right in front of the house. She crosses the street too hastily and gets run over by a car. She is hurt so severely that for a while it is not certain whether she will survive or not. Right away, Puschel is at her best as nurse, friend, and "vice-sister." She contacts us at home and asks us to pray and to publish the events on her website. And she keeps watch at Whitney's hospital bed day and night.

December 23rd, 2006 – Whitney got into a serious accident three days ago. It still is so confusing. Father, I am so, so grateful that she survived. She is in the hospital now and there are a few complications. Father, she is in Your hand. I don't have much to say about this. Let her heal quickly and grant the doctors and people in charge wisdom to do the right thing. Help us to concentrate on You as we go through these next days not knowing what tomorrow holds. Grant us peace in You, and help us to be ever conscious that You are God. Bless Sharon and Gary and grant them peace.

She barely talks about her own pain secretly growing within her. When it becomes worse, she sees doctors in San Salvador. They suspect a herniated disk, so Puschel doesn't worry.... Besides, this Christmas time is about Whitney. Over and over again, Puschel contacts us, asking us to please pray for Whit because she needs it urgently. Of course, we do pray!

Whitney herself writes about this time:
Being her friend meant that she was always there for you. Close to the end of Puschel's time in El Salvador, I had a major accident. I was hit by a car while crossing the street in front of my house. During my stay in the hospital and even throughout my recovery at home, Puschel was there by my side. She spent many nights in the hospital with me and helped me with anything I could not do on my own. Puschel was always there to encourage me to keep going and to never give up on getting better. I will always remember the things she did for me and for everyone else.

January 14th, 2007 – *Time goes by... thank you that Whitney is much better. She is already walking a few steps now. We are allowed to change her bandages at home. Help us to do it all correctly. Father, I want to live all of my life in gratitude. Thank you for saving me and giving me a free entry to eternal life. I want to tell many more people about this "free pass," and I want even more that many will join that journey. Grant us Your joy on this journey* ☺.

By now there are more and more days and nights that Puschel cannot sit anymore, often cannot sleep anymore, and then has to walk around all night for the pain in her pelvis to be bearable. On February 8th, she confides in her journal for the first time how much pain she is in.

She surely told God about the pain earlier. Other than that, she is comforted and encouraged through worship music and the assurance of the Bible. A lot of times she spends all night walking through the house with earphones in her ear and her iPod in her pocket. She doesn't mention any of this to us because she doesn't want us to worry.

Family Holmer in El Salvador

During this time we are filled with joy and excitement for the upcoming weeks. For the three of us (Puschel's younger brother Silas, Eva-Maria, and I) are going to visit Puschel on the other continent. We have been walking in her tracks for a while now. Ever since she was in Aidlingen, our young people drive down for the annual Pentecost youth retreat. We also visit her in Sweden, of course – the end result being that we regularly take our youth there to participate in retreats and form many new friendships. Through that, we create a friendly bond with "Bodenseehof," the Torchbearer center in Friedrichshafen, Germany. This is where Puschel's younger sister gets the chance for an apprenticeship. She worked there for 7 years.

In the beginning of 2007, we are about to follow Puschel's tracks overseas and into the USA. Via New York, we first visit Liesl and her family. We meet a lot of Puschel's other friends, too, and are amazed at how outgoing our daughter, the "plain Jane" of school times, has become. But with all the fun we have in the USA, we are especially excited for our visit at La Casa de Mi Padre in San Salvador. As we touch down at the airport in our Idaho winter clothing and step out of the airplane, heat hits us. From northern winters to the heat of Central America!

In San Salvador we have got one week to get to know Puschel's

Gary Powell and two of his fosterlings

75

work and passion. During that week we get a sense of how deeply she has identified with her work and what a valuable member of the team she has become by now. We spend wonderful moments with Puschel, "her children," and her "second family," the Powell's.

They live in a house that's typical for the area, though probably a little better situated than most of the other ordinary people. There are several employees in the Powell's household who are happy to have a job. Puschel tells us that it was hard for her to be served at first, but since she is so involved in her work at La Casa, she doesn't mind being served at home anymore. Puschel always kindly thanks the servants when they bring her washed laundry or hand her a plate. They in turn seem to appreciate that.

We are allowed to watch our eldest daughter a bit, as she communicates with hands and feet with the kids, and laughs and plays with them. Meanwhile, Puschel does her job. She is sorting through the current medications and is arranging them in the "poison cabinet" in such a way that those in charge can better access them. At the same time she explains to the children how important it is to use one's own cup when drinking water. Because of the heat, they always have water jugs standing around that everyone can drink from. Until now, the children have all used the same cup to drink from, which spreads germs and infections quickly.

The week flies by way too quickly. We had originally planned to drive west to the ocean with Puschel and the Powell's. But we have to cancel those plans because Puschel cannot sit for that long. Her right leg is in too much pain.

We realize that Puschel is not indifferent about saying goodbye to us. It's only later that we realize part of that is the increasing pain in her leg. But at this point we assume that everything will be all right with that. After our departure, Puschel takes care of her duties at La Casa with all of her strength. She can only walk very slowly now and has a hard time concentrating, as she often doesn't sleep for a few nights in a row. A few of the staff members think she is pretending to be in pain and they let her know that. But Puschel would never pretend.

February 25th, 2007 – *Oh my Father, how much do I thank You for the past week. It wasn't an easy one, and I often didn't understand this world, but I am grateful for my time with You. And I know this is only the beginning. Last night when You woke me up during the song, "God, Show Me the Way," after I had* listened to 18 other songs while half asleep (I was searching in vain for that song from last week), I realized that we were going to start a new journey together. And I know, Father, I say so much and do so little. I want to do Your will, listen to You, seek You – You shall be my everything. Nothing and nobody shall ever be more important. You know about my leg, Lord. It is Yours. If I am supposed to lay here for a few more weeks, then Lord, it is Yours. Keep working on me. I want to be of use for You.

February 26th, 2007 – *Psalm 23: I memorized this Psalm years ago as a Christmas gift for my dad. Even then, it impressed and shaped me more than any other part of the Bible at that time. Today You awoke it anew in me. Jesus, You know exactly what my heart needs. When I ask for You and seek You, You will give me whatever I need because then my heart is open for You to fill it. I never want to let go of You – never! You made me whole again on the cross a long time ago and have taken my burden upon You. What great love is this! I imagine that picture right now. A white sheep in a green meadow, the sun is shining and immerses everything in cleanliness, warmth, and peace. This is me when I rest in You! I want You to always guide me because then I will know what is right and what You wish for with all Your heart. And if I am attacked then, Lord, I will not have any reason to fear… for You are there and have long ago won the fight. I can hide behind You just like Fridolin[38] hid behind me when he was afraid. I can and want to live in the knowledge of Your unconditional love for me and of You always wanting the best for my life. I have the certainty that I am Your little lamb which You watch over joyfully.*
Today I realized why I have never missed anything in Your presence. I mean, You have always blessed me. Even when I had hard times in my life (and there are a lot of people who have harder lives…), You turned them into a blessing. I want to dwell in the house of the Lord forever![39] Amen.

---

[38] The lamb Puschel bottle-fed.
[39] Psalm 27:4.

My Life is in Your Hands!

It is the end of February 2007. We are back home. We were aware that Puschel was in a great deal of pain and we even gave her a pain shot. But what's really causing it, nobody knows at this point.

February 27th, 2007 – *In the darkest valley You are with us.*[40] *My Father, when I walk through the valley of death, You are even closer to hold me in Your hand. You have already conquered those places of death. You know them. My life is in Your* *hands. And I trust that You will not for-* *The diagnosis reads* *sake me in the darkest times. You have* *"herniated disk"* *Your reasons for not leading me around* *the darkness but instead, through it. Your plans are perfect. You are the Lord of time and eternity. One day I will be allowed to be with You in eternity. What surety! Even here on earth You give me a sense of what's to come. Thank you for Your love for me personally.*

Puschel is seeking medical help in El Salvador, one of the poorest countries in Central America. In fact, she is being checked with the only MRI in the country. The problem, however, is that nobody seems to be able to read the results properly. The doctors' diagnosis is a herniated disk. They recommend surgery, but that would best be done in Buenos Aires, Argentina, or Santiago de Chile, not in El Salvador. A hospital in the United States is eliminated from the list because of the costs. Puschel turns to doctors in the States who have a friendly association with La Casa and also sends the MRI results to her Uncle "Lumpi," my younger brother, Traugott, who is a neurologist in Zurich. He and the American colleagues agree that she does not need surgery, and that it most likely is not a herniated disk either. While Puschel tries to continue her work at the orphanage, which is a challenge since every movement hurts, we talk to the insurance company and call doctors in Germany.

March 3rd, 2007 – *My Father, thank you for Your hug this morning. Today is Saturday. I met doctors who want to help me loosen up my back to finally reduce the pain a bit. Bless the time*

---

[40] Psalm 23:4

I am going to have with Kevin, who is supposed to help me. Father, thank you for the reminder that You love me unconditionally, and that I am loved here on earth. Being with You is the best place on earth. I didn't deserve it, but You cleansed me and dressed me with a new robe so I can be in Your presence – all because You love me. Why would I want to be more than Your daughter who is unconditionally loved? Daughter of the King, the Creator of heaven and earth. It is unbelievable. You are love! I inherited it. I want to pass it along, to carry on that inheritance.

March 22nd, 2007 – *Father, thank you for the angel who donated the money for the salaries! Thank you for Your guidance today. Father, You clearly lead us. Thank you for opening my eyes for that today. Thank you for this day. I entrust my friends/family here to You and ask You to be the only one in charge. To You be the glory and praise forever.*

March 31st, 2007 – *Let us fix our eyes on Jesus, the author and perfecter.... Hebrews 12:2. What a Father I have! Lord, do not let me forget that. I want to walk upright through this dark world in order to pass on Your light. I might have to leave this country next week. Lord, prevent that if it is not Your will. However, if Your plan is for me to continue in Germany, I want to follow that happily.*

Return Flight First Class

The question of how to help Puschel becomes more and more pressing for us. Shall we bring her back to Germany to get her a definitive diagnosis? Finally the insurance is approved: we are bringing her back. A doctor flies to San Salvador to ensure a safe and smooth return of the patient and to accompany her. When Puschel hears about this, she prays: Lord, let this man be blessed through this trip. The doctor becomes acquainted with the work of La Casa after his arrival there and is very impressed. So much so that he is about to adopt one of the kids.

Puschel had allowed her original return ticket to go unused since she had wanted to stay in El Salvador. She is now flying home first class for free. She would have gladly forgone that luxury, but now this is exactly what she needs as she cannot sit for long periods of time. Even though she has a comfortable and spacious accommodation, she has to walk around quite a bit as she cannot stay in one position for very long. The doctor already realizes on the return trip that it was high time to get Puschel back home. Back in Germany she loses touch with the doctor. However, she keeps praying for him often. Puschel does not know if she will return to El Salvador one day. She does now know, however, that it was not a mistake to have gone there without formal preparations. Had she gone through culture and language training with a missionary agency, her departure would have been months later. Her pain would already have appeared during the preparation time already. No agency would have sent her out under such circumstances, which would have meant she never would have gone to El Salvador. In hindsight, her seemingly carefree way of thinking to go without any formal training was exactly the right thing for her to do.

Back in Germany

The Diagnosis

As soon as Puschel gets back to Germany, she is admitted to a specialized hospital in Plau am See (Mecklenburg), about 50 kilometers[41] from Bülow. They want to examine her thoroughly. Puschel is admitted for in-patient care, and we visit her that first night. Based on the diagnosis in El Salvador, her vertebral disks get scanned and examined first. But the doctors determine immediately that the disks are not the problem. Early the following week, her pelvis is supposed to get scanned. Meanwhile, they let Puschel go home for the weekend. We are excited to have her home – after all, she has been on the other side of the globe for a year.

On Monday, she has to go back to Plau. We already get a call that afternoon and are asked to come to the hospital for a conversation with the chief physician. This cannot be good. We parents sit down at the kitchen table together, fold our hands in prayer, and put the upcoming hours before God. We know that both we and Puschel are held in His almighty hands, and nothing will happen that isn't part of His plans. Since we already know that we can bring Puschel home after the conversation, Eva-Maria stays home to get everything ready while I drive to Plau. Sitting in the car, I can't stop my mind from racing through all kinds of scenarios. But it is no use to ponder.

Then I am sitting in the senior physician's office, while Puschel is told to wait in her room. The doctor sits across from me behind his desk, props his elbows up on the table, folds his hands and says:

He avoids the words cancer and tumor

"Mr. Holmer, what we found in Your daughter's pelvis is relatively obvious. Something is growing there that does not belong…." I understand. My thoughts start racing. The doctor does not mention the words cancer or tumor, but they are spinning through my head. He wants to clarify that for now I should not tell my daughter about the whole situation. We should tell her gently that hard times lay

---

[41] About 31 miles

ahead. Meanwhile, he would try to get us connected to one of the specialized tumor centers in Germany.

My thoughts are still spinning. I am not sure where they come from or where they are going. But my answer baffles him, and it throws him off: "Doctor, I most certainly will tell my daughter what is going on because she is a person who absolutely relies on God. She knows that everything in her life is in God's hand."

I thank him, step out of the room, and close the door behind me.

Her grandpa doesn't let her go without a prayer

My steps echo through the hospital corridor. I am trying to sort through my thoughts. When I step into Puschel's room and meet her eyes, I realize that she is not as clueless as the doctor has thought. After all she did her apprenticeship and worked in one of the biggest pediatric oncology hospitals in Germany.

"Dad, you don't have to say anything…" she says. She just wants to go home.

Just as we finish up gathering up her things, a nurse approaches us and asks us to come back to the chief physician's office. He has already talked to a specialty clinic and made an appointment for the day after tomorrow. Puschel says goodbye to him. "I know that it is serious, doctor. But I also know that God always wants the best for us." I can tell the doctor is struggling to retain his composure, and he says goodbye quickly. We may contact him anytime if we have any problems anywhere or with anything. A few minutes later we are in the car.

Trust starts where understanding and knowledge cease

I start driving, shift, signal, steer. We stop to buy something. I don't remember what it was. Everything is blurry and unimportant. Puschel wants to stop at her grandpa's on the way to at least briefly say hi. She knows that he won't let her go without praying together and blessing her. I cannot really remember that visit. I only remember that I called my wife at some point and told her what the doctor had said. She had suspected it.

The next thing that happened, about two hours later, I can still vividly recall today. Puschel and I are standing at my office window looking out at the "Mecklenburgische Schweiz"[42] and the big

---

[42] Translated: "Mecklenburg Switzerland - this region is so called so because it is the most beautiful and lovely region of Mecklenburg (like Switzerland in the view of all Europe).

church property that stretches to the shore of the lake "Malchiner See." I am standing next to my daughter, fighting an incredible lump in my throat while my eyes burn. Puschel's eyes are wet, too. But then she says something in a slightly shaky voice, words that she later writes in her journal:

Dad, I have a deep inner peace in my heart because I know nothing happens without God's approval. I know His plan is perfect. I know for sure that He means well and that He will do things well. Jesus gave me a very deep inner peace in my heart. Whatever comes next, He will be there. My biggest sadness would be if this broke you and Mom. Your sadness and despair would drain me most. I want you both to feel the same deep inner peace that I have.

Now I am the one who is baffled and doesn't know what to say. Thoughts run through my head: "Oh God, how can this be? Help us to trust You and feel secure in Your mighty hands." It is one thing to believe in God, yet another to trust Him fully.

Trust starts where understanding and knowledge cease, because this is when we see how much we trust in God's paths and whether that trust sustains us. That sustained Puschel from the beginning. We are just starting to learn. She is absolutely assured that God's plan is perfect, and nothing can separate her from the love of God which we find in Jesus (Romans 8:39). Her trust makes it easier for us to walk with her on this journey.

This is the start of a time that shapes our lives so tremendously that, in the end, we do not want to miss these experiences, for God made us grow strong in our relationship with Him. Nobody would ever wish for a time or situation like this. For us it becomes the most intense[43] time of our lives thus far.

God's Big Family

Theoretically, we always knew what it meant to be a child of God and a member of His huge family here on earth. However, it never before had such a deep meaning in our lives. This changes abruptly now. Modern technology suddenly becomes very personal

---

[43] A time with an extremely large number of spiritual and human experiences within a short period.

and has an almost existential meaning for us: Puschel's website becomes a way of informing and updating friends and family all over the world about her illness. Our family is big and everyone, of course, wants to know how she is doing. Now they can inform themselves via the website, and we don't have to call each person and each time repeat what is going on. This is especially difficult because of the fat lump we often feel in our throats.... From the beginning, it goes for Puschel really hard.

April 22nd, 2007 she writes her first internet letter since returning to Germany:

My dear friends, I cannot really describe the deep inner peace, joy, strength, and hope I am filled with. In terms of me as a human being and of my health, it looks pretty dark right now! But this is not all bad. I can see how God is drawing many hearts closer right now. I know His plan is perfect (even if we cannot always understand it – Jeremiah 29:11). Physically I am often tired; I cannot do much. At least I understand now why I have been so tired over the past few months. My leg is getting worse, but I am getting good medication. Thank you all for all the prayers and support. May God bless you. I will keep you posted. ~Puschel

A Difficult Path
is Coming

Prayer for Puschel

W e find ourselves praying a lot during the following days. In one of the neighboring villages, the staff of "Word of Life"[44] is leading a Bible study. On April 27th, an evening bonfire is on the schedule. Members of the Bible study, the "Word of Life" staff, and a group from our church sit in a circle, deep in thought, as they stare into the crackling fire. It is an odd, rather quiet atmosphere, because Puschel is there, too. Her diagnosis is like the sword of Damocles hovering over her head, and over all of us. We start to pray, one after the other, with and for Puschel. The next day we have a visit from Serrahn – Grandpa Holmer, my brother Markus, his wife Elke, and several of our church elders. We want to anoint Puschel with oil and pray for her as instructed in James 5:13-18. With our prayer, we want to confirm our trust in God and in His Word. As we part ways, we know that we all – especially Puschel – are heading into a future where we can only trust in God's promises. God assures us that He will always be with us. Puschel especially clings to that promise. From that time on, she does not ever let go of that trust.

Unknown Terrain

On Monday, April 30th, 2007, Puschel, Eva-Maria, and I are on our way to the specialty clinic. We do not talk much. The world we now enter is too unfamiliar. Fortunately, Puschel and I are people who can accept things as they are and face them step by step as they come. That is much harder for Eva-Maria. She thinks a lot, wondering what could happen. However, had we known what was to come, we probably would not have left the house that day…. We are registered at the specialty clinic and have an appointment for today.

---

[44] A large youth mission organization originally based in America

However, nobody takes notice when we arrive. It is a cold clinic building from the early 20th century that survived World War II and the GDR era. In the GDR, the clinic was considered one of the top oncology and specialty clinics. But nothing is modern here anymore, especially not the structure itself. We stand around in the hallway, a little lost – ordered to come, but now with no one to meet us. Patients listlessly shuffle past us. Two nurses push an empty bed through the hall. We cannot find anyone in charge. Puschel's eyes are teary as she says, "Dad, we are not going to stay here. We should find a different clinic." Eva-Maria suggests, "Let's go to the park, talk to God, and then call the chief doctor in Plau am See. He registered us for this visit, and he said we could call anytime if we needed help." So, we walk through the park, stop suddenly near a bench, and pray: "Lord, You brought us here. Please take care of us. We are dependent on You. Please!" Someone walks by and looks at us blankly. But we know that God hears our prayers. Then we call the chief doctor in Plau. None of us have ever been seriously sick, which is why we are inexperienced. We don't know much, including the things God is arranging behind the scenes.

Finally Some Advice

When we walk back to the clinic, we meet a friendly man who addresses us directly, "Can I help you in any way?"

"We are thinking about looking for a different hospital," we reply. "We have the impression that things are not very structured here." He listens to us and then asks us to sit down in a corner of the hallway and wait for a few minutes. He would be back shortly and try to help us.

We wait and wait, thinking, well that figures. But then he comes back as promised, sits down, apologizes for the wait, and explains, "I was looking at the results of the examinations in Plau am See, so it took a little longer than expected." He apologizes that he has to talk to us in the hallway. "We don't even have a free doctor's room to quietly have a proper consultation." Then he introduces himself. "I am senior physician, Dr. T. I completely understand. If you really would like to find a different hospital, I will try to assist you, as I know important people at several tumor centers. I will try to clarify and answer all your questions now, however." He patiently and empathetically explains how things stand for Puschel. What he says sounds concrete and threatening. There can be no doubts. There definitely is a tumor in her right pelvis that keeps eating its way into the bone. Surgery? Dr. T. considers surgery her only option. This would mean the whole tumor needs to be removed from the healthy tissue, as far as that is possible. The surgery must be preceded with chemotherapy to reduce the size of the tumor and help isolate it from the surrounding healthy tissue.

It is a very long consultation. It shows us, however, that there is a man here who seems to know what he is doing and who can make suggestions. So we soon decide to stay here. Later, other things seem friendlier than they appeared during this first visit.

The chemo is supposed to start in only a few days. We have no alternative. So we drive back north, reconciled with the situation but seeing the dark prospects. Two days *It is definitely a* later, Puschel's Uncle Lumpi visits. He is *tumor* a neurologist in a clinic in Switzerland. He wants to take time with Puschel, answer any remaining questions, and encourage and comfort her. They go on walks together through the blooming fields and meadows of Mecklenburg.

When he has to leave, he says goodbye and tells us, "Don't make a lot of plans. It is going to be a long and hard road. At some point you will run out of strength, so you need to pace yourselves. In the beginning, everything is new. But at some point, Puschel, you will be the leader of the dance. You will know what is right for you better than any doctor...."

Later on, we often have to remember his words. It is true; Puschel soon knows her illness very well. But in one thing he was wrong – she never loses her strength. She experiences how "His power is made perfect in weakness" (2 Corinthians 12:9) and knows that a lot of friends pray for her intensely.

Under an "Unlucky Star"?

The conditions for the upcoming weeks are - from a human point of view - very poor. The update on her website for friends and prayer partners reads as follows:

Our dear friends! The results of the tissue samples are here. However, it is worse than we had expected or feared. Puschel has stage 3 chondrosarcoma, which means it is the worst possible diagnosis. Her pelvic bone is completely infiltrated by the tumor. She is facing an extremely difficult surgery. Before that, she will get chemotherapy (which is only effective in about 30% of cases for this kind of cancer) to try to prevent the cancer cells from spreading elsewhere. Today and tomorrow, she will be at home; Thursday morning she has to go back to the hospital. If you are willing and able, please pray that she might enjoy the two days at home and then be at peace as she approaches the chemotherapy and its side effects. And because we know our God, we also know that HE can heal her. Please pray that HE may glorify Himself through her. Thank you!

At this point Puschel still has the strength to write to her friends via the internet herself:

May 2nd, 2007 – Oh friends, how you have uplifted and encouraged me throughout the past two weeks! Thank you for all your prayers and intercessions to God – and some of you even fasted!! Thank you for all your emails. Thank you for your time and for thinking of me! HIS peace is within me; may it also be within you! The upcoming period is not going to be easy for me. But HE is with me. And you, too, are with me on this journey. Thank you for fighting with me! (Read 2 Corinthians 1:3-11). I asked the doctors to give me two days at home before the chemo starts. I could tell you a lot about the last week. But I do not have the strength for that right now. I can only tell you that God is simply holding and carrying me. However, I am going to get a bit heavier for Him in the next few days... (not really, because He is God!!) But I know He can uphold me, and He will! I was especially happy about my Uncle Lumpi's visit from Switzerland. He is a doctor and came to the hospital for three days, and he also escorted me home. He could answer and explain a lot of the medical questions. That did me good. My pain is much more under control and much better than the past three months as well.

Let me briefly explain the doctors' next plans. (At the same time, I am certain God's plan is going to look a bit different. He likes taking different routes. They are the best, even if we don't always understand!)

A small surgery is scheduled for Friday, in which I am getting a so-called port that is planted under the skin below my shoulder. The port will lead into my vein and thus into my blood stream and is used to administer the chemotherapy. This is going

I know God
will uphold me

to simplify the process, since an access through the arm veins would be more cumbersome and would have to be put in place each time. With the port, there is also less danger of infection. The chemo is supposed to start on Saturday. It will last three to five days, depending on the kind of medicine. If I feel well enough and am stable, I can go home for a week after that. This is going to go on for 10 weeks, with different kinds of drugs and breaks in between. A big surgery is scheduled after all of that. Once that is over and I am stable enough, chemotherapy will continue for ten months altogether. That's the plan of the doctors – as I said, the doctors. What God does is not written in this plan.... Now I have a verse for you that is worth meditating on – Isaiah 41:10 [NIV]: "So do not fear, for I am with you; do not be dismayed, for I am your God. I will strengthen you and help you; I will uphold you with my righteous right hand." Lastly, I had a moment of delight today. My brother Silas and my mother picked up four lambs that are now running around on our property; this was the first winter since I can remember that we did not have sheep ....

It's Getting Down to the Nitty-gritty

The first minor surgery goes smoothly. Puschel gets a port. At the same time her pain medications are getting better adjusted, which leads to nausea (as expected) until her body gets used to the drugs. In the beginning she also gets a pain patch. Only a few hours later she has to vomit – the dosage of the pain patch was set too high. Everything is prepared now. On the morning of May 4th, Puschel gets her first chemo treatment. She is placed in a four-bed room with three older ladies in the old hospital building. That, however, proves to be rather problematic, because Puschel has an extremely strong reaction to this first chemotherapy treatment. She develops a strong sensitivity to light and noise. Even the nurses who have worked here in GDR times have never experienced such. But they would not adjust anything.

Puschel must stay in that room. An older deaf lady continuously speaks very loudly on the phone so we have to plug Puschel's ears. In addition, she puts a pillow over her ears because she seems to perceive every noise a hundredfold. Due to her light hypersensitivity, we place a wet washcloth over her closed eyes and her forehead which also brings her a little moisture and freshness. Puschel has to throw up. Repeatedly. We realize that she is not entirely with us anymore; she almost seems to be comatose. As I walk down the hall to get a bottle of water, I pass by the nurses' station and overhear them talking about Puschel – "Lydia is a sniveling, sensitive baby who is crying for mama and papa." From that day on, she gets stuck with that label. The first chemo treatment is supposed to take one week.

During that time, we stay with friends who live close by. After three days, Eva-Maria takes over sitting next to Puschel. I have to go back home to attend to my duties as a pastor. We are already pushing the limit – or so we think. Puschel does not notice much anymore. Later she tells us that she can barely remember anything about this first chemo treatment. That's how much this chemotherapy is putting her into some sort of blackout.

On the evening of May 9th, I am sitting at home preparing the next church service and am struggling to concentrate. A thick lump is forming in my throat as I think about my daughter in that hospital and my wife, Eva-Maria.

I pray again and again. At 9 PM, Eva-Maria says goodnight to our friends. I keep working. It is far past midnight, and suddenly my cell phone rings. It is a doctor from the hospital. "Mr. Holmer, I was trying to reach your wife. She was here yesterday." I tell him, "You cannot talk with her right now. I hope she is fast asleep." The doctor replies, "Then we need to talk. We should think about doing something for Your daughter. She desperately needs a psychotherapist to talk to. She is barely responsive."

I am getting furious. We already heard that they think she is a sniveling baby, and now she is supposedly also mentally unstable. We know that Puschel is not an over-reactive, over-sensitive person. I tell the doctor, "Do you know what my daughter needs? Nothing but her home, her familiar surroundings, and simply peace and quiet. Yes, right now she is hypersensitive to light and noise. However, that is not because she likes it or because she is sniveling, but because all of this obviously drains her physically. Psychologically

– and I am 100% sure of that – she is absolutely fine. I ask you to do whatever necessary to discharge her as soon as possible. She is only in the hospital for observation purposes now anyway."

A Different Birthday Present

Under these circumstances, I am not even aware that this is my 50th birthday. However, I get a birthday present of a very special kind. The previous night the doctor told me that Lydia had to stay in the hospital for observation at least until 11:00. Yet the next morning, everything goes really fast. When Eva-Maria gets to the hospital, the nurses tell her that Lydia can go home right away. While Eva-Maria packs up her stuff, Puschel is pushed into the hallway. She is supposed to wait there for her medical report and her transportation home.

Eva-Maria notices that Puschel's spot is given to a new patient only half an hour later. They needed room. It still takes hours until the ambulance arrives. In the afternoon my birthday present is "de-

May 10th, 2007 – Puschel is back from her first chemotherapy round but now she must go to the next hospital that same night. Friend, Lucia, is sitting with her.

livered" to Bülow. We are extremely grateful and enjoy a different kind of birthday party.

A Completely Different Treatment

Puschel is now lying in her own bed but still barely responsive. We take care of her as best we can. Suddenly, she develops a fever, one that keeps going up. Finally, we have no option but to call the hospital in Teterow, which is 12 kilometers (about 7.5 miles) away. They quickly send an emergency doctor. Puschel is taken to the hospital immediately; this time it's a small one that is definitely not equipped for this kind of thing. Nevertheless, they take good care of her. She is put into a big double room, which allows one of us to be with her at all times. They prescribe absolute silence when anyone is with her and put a sign on her door. The chief physician is not a specialist in oncology, but he quickly realizes that Puschel is completely dehydrated. Puschel is unable to drink, but her port allows them to hook up an IV bag. We are relieved that Puschel is being well cared for now. The next day, her friend Myriam, from southern Germany, is coming to be with her for a few days. That frees us up a little.

After a few days, Puschel comes to herself again and realizes that she does not remember much about the events of the last few days. Her smile left her face for a little while, but now it returns. It takes a few more days before she is released to go home again. So, my 50th birthday becomes a celebration after all, even if a little belated. At the very least, I will surely never forget it. When Puschel finally gets home, she knows that there are hospitals out there where people treat you in a friendly manner.

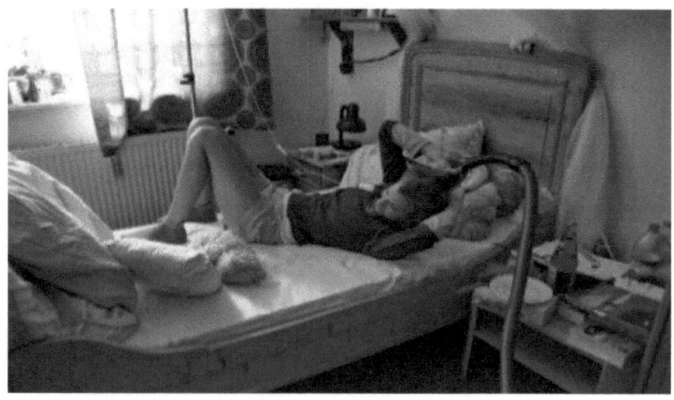

Puschel takes it with humor. Her hair gets removed by the vacuum.

Puschel writes to her friends on the internet:

My dear friends, I know that I have to rest a lot, but I cannot wait any longer – I want to write you all a short message at least. During the past two weeks I've had a lot of tears in my eyes because I was so touched by the fact that I have a huge "heavenly" family. I am sooooo grateful for your prayers. Thank you for all your emails and letters. I have a map in my room on which I can see all the countries where I have friends who are praying for me (El Salvador, Nicaragua, Argentina, USA, Canada, New Zealand, Australia, China, Latvia, Sweden, Netherlands, Belgium, Austria, Switzerland, Poland, Germany). A lot has happened over the last two weeks. However, if I am honest, I cannot remember much. I just read the reports my dad posted during those days. I can only tell you that God carried me through that time.

I can remember lying in Teterow. My body was so weak that I couldn't even drink anything by myself. Oftentimes, I wasn't even able to think about my situation. One time, however, I thought that this could have been the end of my life here on earth. I told God then that I would like to stay a little longer. But if His will is different, then it would be okay, too, because my life does not belong to me but to Him. For a few days it seemed like only Jesus was there, and me (not my body). The only thing that mattered was HIM. It is really hard to explain, but that's how it was. I know more clearly than ever before: when I have to go, I am going to an even better place.

Please don't think I am tired of my life, however. I just wanted to share about the peace I feel and that nothing can separate my Lord and me unless I consciously make that decision. However, the decision to turn against God would be the dumbest thing I could ever do. Because I am nothing without Him, yet He is everything for me! My friends, all we need is Jesus! I know that there are a lot of problems in life but I want to encourage you to always turn to Him.

"This poor man called, and the Lord heard him; He saved him out of all his troubles." – Psalm 34:6 [NIV]. Let us walk boldly and "collect" His promises and take Him at His word. Let God really be God! He is the Creator.

Who do you know who is bigger than He is and wants to accompany you your whole life? Let's focus on Him! Let Him be your teacher and form you! He wants to take you by the hand! My dad's last report about my hair is right. I can pull on it and give it to my visitors in bunches. But that's okay. Regarding beauty, I will probably have to yield precedence to the other girls…. (My dad thinks I am beautiful without hair as well! He told me…!) Just wait until my first "Puschel curls" start growing again….

Puschel takes it all in stride with her own kind of humor. She does not have a problem getting her picture taken while she is "taking off" her hair with the vacuum cleaner. She loses her hair but not her beauty. Many pictures on her internet page bear witness to it: her happiness, her gratitude, and her charisma remain.

A Church Bell for San Salvador

Puschel often talks on the phone with Gary Powell in El Salvador. He, his family, and many of the staff members want to know how Puschel is doing. Gary encourages her and tells her that her friends regularly meet up to read the Bible and pray for her. Gary also reports on the progress at the orphanage. He is planning to build houses for the children on a farm that is already owned by La Casa. First, he would like to build a chapel; the construction plans were just finished. Gary asks Puschel whether there is something that should not be missing in that chapel. Puschel doesn't think long about it and says, "The chapel absolutely needs a bell." "A bell?"

Puschel knows that only a few churches in Central America have church bells. Most are only equipped with tiny bells. Puschel, however, is thinking of a big and heavy bell. It is not until she hangs up that she realizes what she has suggested. "Papa, what do you think? How could we get a bell for the chapel?" We come up with the idea of asking all of our friends to financially support the project – "A bell for La Casa." When Puschel proposes her idea on her website, she immediately gets a lot of approving emails.

You've heard of the bell for La Casa de Mi Padre. Thank you so much for all your responses. My dad will tell You how You can get involved if you would like to help. (Entry in the internet)

In a short amount of time, Puschel's friends donate enough money to order a small new bell to be poured. Three months later, we pick up the bell in Bavaria. Unfortunately, Puschel cannot come with us as she is getting chemotherapy again and needs to rest in between. While we are building the shipping box, Puschel's little brother, Silas, hangs the bell on a new roof on our property. That way Puschel is the first one to ring the bell and hear its chimes across the meadows and our village.

From then on, she can only follow the transportation to the harbor in Hamburg by looking at pictures. When the bell gets shipped and hung up in El Salvador, Gary records the sounds of the first time it chimes. That bell chime can now be heard every time someone clicks on the subpage "La Casa" on her internet website. Puschel is beyond happy and excited to share this with her friends and thank them for their love and support. More important to her than that, however, is the work of "La Casa" and their vision. The bell itself is just an additional "call of the gospel" to the vicinity.

I would like to ask you to look at the homepage of "MFH" – *https://www.mfh-elsalvador.org*. You can read about their vision and everything concerning the children. That is exactly what is on my heart most – children without parents. I want nothing more than for them to learn about the Father in heaven and His family here on earth. The whole project is still in the beginning phase. It is a project that not only works with the kids but also with their relatives.

A Tricky Situation

The most important thing for Puschel now is getting her prepared for the big surgery in August. A part of those preparations are the rounds of chemotherapy that are supposed to reduce the size of the tumor and isolate it in order to remove it more easily. Yet the chemotherapy weakens Puschel, her immune system, and her organ functions. That does not help the conditions for such a big surgical procedure. It is a tricky situation, but we do not have a choice.

June 17th, 2007 – Puschel writes: *My dear friends, thank you for all your emails, letters, and prayers. Thank you for all the encouraging words, Bible verses and songs. Some of you wrote: "The only thing I can do for you is pray...." I can only tell you that prayer is the best you can do for me! What could be better than putting your loved ones into the hands of God?! One of His biggest promises is that He will hear us! The thing I am "allowed" to learn every single day anew is rejoicing with and in Him. His invitation not to worry (Matthew 6:34) is more a command than a suggestion. When we start to worry, we let our problems become bigger than God.*

Let me tell you about my last chemo. God "allowed" me to leave the hospital with more energy than I had when I entered it. Thank you so much for your prayers! Oh, and yesterday, after two days break at home, I went back to the hospital with my dad and my friend Eva. After we took care of all the paperwork, the blood samples, and everything else you have to do at admission, we were able to enjoy a little walk outside together. I asked Jesus to show us a good pizza restaurant nearby so we might enjoy a hearty meal. You know what? I think I enjoyed the best pizza of my life that night! God takes care of the smallest details! As I am typing this letter to you, the chemo that I did not tolerate at all the first time, is dripping into my body. This time it is different. I am so grateful for my current state. I happily enjoyed the last piece of pizza before the chemo this morning and am eating a piece of watermelon right now.

My pain has decreased even within the past two weeks. It cannot be compared at all to the pain I had in the five months prior. But I also know that God will carry me in case I am starting to feel lousy again. He always has. How wonderful to know that my future lies in His hands! As I am writing this, I am already past the last day of the rough, final chemo of this cycle. I am so grateful that I am still feeling so well. My pain has gotten better also. It is pretty different than the past two weeks. I am so grateful to know that my Father in heaven is holding my future in His hand! Okay, and now I need to take a little nap....

More and more people use Puschel's website to get an update on her illness and her current state. Often several hundred people a day. Most of them pray for her. Many write to her, too. That is a huge encouragement to Puschel because it takes its toll on her, humanly and emotionally, more than it seems from the outside. Her biggest joy is knowing that so many people turn to Jesus every day and talk to Him.

In the following weeks, Puschel's skin starts to tear open

because of the chemo. Some of those tears on her feet, that do not seem to want to heal, are becoming a new risk we are not yet aware of.

On July 15th, she really wants to go home because there is a music youth festival in Bülow, the so-called "Pommfest," that she really does not want to miss. Nothing is more important to Puschel than for youth to learn about Jesus. She prays in the hospital in Berlin for those festival days. She really wants to participate as well. However! She is actually getting released from the hospital that day after another tough chemo round. Yet everything turns out differently.

The next day, Puschel's friends read on her page:

Last night, Puschel suddenly got a fever; a high, too high of a fever. In the end she was at 40,2°C.[45]

That was too much and happened too quickly. We thus had to take Puschel back to the hospital in Teterow that very night.

Everyone there was sooo nice to her and to us. But we only had three hours of rest when they decided she needed to be transferred to Berlin. We had to pack her things for Berlin quickly even though she had been so excited to come home. So, we hope and pray that the physicians will get this infection, or whatever it is, under control quickly, and that she can come home again soon. We are sooooo grateful to our God for the great medical care we get in our country. But even all those medical options reach their limits quickly. So, we must keep interceding and praying. And if you would like to join us, we would be so grateful to God and you.

Puschel has severe blood poisoning, which can only be treated by intensive care measures, since her body is extremely weakened by the last chemo treatment. We, of course, often talk about the right arrangements. We often wonder if all of this is right. But nobody can really tell what is right. We are dependent on the advice and the knowledge of the doctors. We have the certainty that, in the end, everything is in God's hand. And thus Puschel, too, is okay with following the doctor's advice.

---

[45] 104.36 Fahrenheit

Miracles One Can See

Meanwhile, life in our family and church community is taking its (almost) normal course. Over and over again, we and Puschel experience incredible things – signals that you would think were sent straight down from heaven.

One Sunday, some of our church members want to pray together for Puschel. I am reluctant as we are talking about my daughter. So, one of the board members of our church council takes the lead on this. But first, I preach the sermon. As I preach, with the church doors open, since it is beautifully sunny outside, a tourist sticks his head into the church to see the almost 800-year-old building. I look at him and invite him to join us. He may go whenever he needs to. He sits down – and stays. During the closing prayer he hears what is said and prayed regarding Puschel.

We exchange a few words at the door, and he leaves. A few days later Puschel gets an email from this very tourist. He tells her that he was in the church and witnessed how the congregation took an active interest in Puschel and prayed for her. He found her website on the internet and is now certain that she is the Lydia whom he had examined in the MRI three months ago in Plau am See – the radiologist in Plau. He had felt sorry then to have to give her such a bad diagnosis, and he had been impressed by how she handled it. He tells her he wants to start praying for her now, too, since so many seem to do that. He says he may not be religious or a believer and wasn't sure whether God accepted his prayers, but he wanted to try it.

Puschel is very touched. She replies – Yes, God hears our prayers, even if we are not sure. She invites him to come back if he gets a chance. Today this young doctor is at home in our church. He has become a Christian, was baptized three years ago, and lives in one of our neighboring villages. Puschel testifies more and more assuredly – I know that God's plan is perfect. That is also supposed to be the title for the article that the evangelical journal, "*IdeaSpektrum*," later published about her.

When Matthias Pankau, the journalist, asks for an interview and comes for a visit, he has one question: Can we publish a story like that before the surgery? Or wouldn't it be better to wait and see how things turn out?

Puschel says, "If my trust in God's good plans was only

sufficient enough to see if things turn out well, it wouldn't be trust. Because if God takes me home through this surgery or something else happens, then that, too, is a good plan." So, the article is published during her time of chemotherapy rounds, which repeatedly bring her to her knees.

Day X Before the Big Surgery

Puschel is still in Berlin, trying to recover from the blood poisoning. She cannot wait to go home. She does not want to spend an extra (unnecessary) day in the hospital! Right before the surgery, the camp for the grandchildren of Grandpa Holmer is starting, and Puschel would really like to catch at least part of it.

About 35 of Grandpa Holmer's grandchildren are attending. The same day, Puschel becomes a proud and grateful aunt, because her older brother Titus becomes a dad! For her, however, it is a back and forth between chemotherapy rounds, blood poisoning, and little breaks in Bülow. From a medical point of view, she is in the best hands in Berlin. It is a newly built and very modern complex. We are grateful to God for that.

However, day X, the day of her surgery, is drawing closer and closer. We do not know what the outcome of the surgery will be. The big tumor in Puschel's pelvis, which is pinching her sciatic nerve and causing her immense pain, is to be completely removed, if possible. Puschel's right fibula is going to be removed and placed into her pelvis for support, while her pelvic bone, where the cancer is, will be taken out. We know this is not going to be easy. But we

Puschel with her family before the big surgery

99

also know that the physicians will do their best, and that God has everything in His hands.

Before the surgery, Puschel posts a letter to her friends on August 15th. It is the last thing she can write herself for the next several weeks:

> *I want to thank those of you again who are praying for my family and me. I wish it was possible for me to thank each and every one of you personally. I am glad and grateful to have been able to spend the past two weeks at home. Every morning it is a fight to get out of bed, because I am so weakened from the chemo. However, when I fall into bed completely exhausted at night, I am so grateful to God for all the awesome things I got to enjoy that day. During the past few weeks, a lot of people asked me how I feel about the surgery, and whether I am scared. I have to say that His peace has not left me. And to be honest, I have not been scared as of now. I am a little nervous but not worried. You know, friends, when I get scared I start looking at the problems. Just like Peter did (Matthew 14:22-36).*
>
> *You know, my doctor told me that my leg will never fully recover after the surgery. That was a shock for me at first. But after I thought and prayed about it, I realized that this, too, is in God's hand ("quick learner" haha), and that God can do much more than we could ever imagine (Ephesians 3:20). If it turns out the way the doctors say, then I do not know why yet, but Jesus does.*

A Welcome Present

When we take Puschel to the Berlin hospital's oncological surgery unit on August 15th, 2007, God gives her a welcome present. At the hospital ward, a nurse named Juergen welcomes us. He tells us that he studied at the Bible institute which was then led by Grandpa Holmer. He then decided that he didn't want to be a preacher and instead became a nurse. He specifically wanted to work in the oncology ward so he could support people in exceptionally hard times. Now he heads the ward and does everything possible to create a pleasant environment. We notice that at every turn. Puschel takes this as a true gift from God.

Eva-Maria and I promised Puschel in the beginning that we

would not leave her alone in the hospitals anymore if it was in our authority to prevent it. We would divide our responsibilities as follows: I go to the hospitals with Puschel and am present at all physician consultations and for important decisions. Eva-Maria prepares everything for Puschel to return home and tends to Puschel's care. I can usually arrange to be off for a few days or take vacation leave. Oftentimes, I have to leave in between to go home for a funeral, a Sunday church service, or a wedding.

Puschel's friend, Myri, cannot stand being in the south anymore and comes to Berlin without hesitation. She rents a room in a little guesthouse so she can be there for Puschel the two days before and during the surgery. Whenever I come with Puschel to Berlin, I am always wonderfully hosted by the young Dehn family in Lobetal. We already knew them from when they were colleagues of my father, when my parents worked in Lobetal, and later when they took in Erich Honecker and his wife.[46]

At the Dehns, I have a real bed as often as I need it. This allows me to drive to the hospital in the mornings and stay as long as I need to, sometimes late into the night. A lot of different examinations are scheduled for this day, and then we are called into the final physician consultation. It is important for Puschel to have at least one of us parents with her for things like that. The physician who is going to do the surgery is the same one who explained everything to us patiently in the beginning and helped us with the difficult situation in the old clinic. He has already shown us detailed images. He made a true scale 3D model of Puschel's pelvis which he calculated by computer using the MRI and CAT scan images. There is a slight hope that the sciatic nerve may be preserved. As we leave the consultation room, we say to him, "We will pray for you, doctor. We know that God can steer and lead all things." He looks at us for a moment, surprised, then says: "Sometimes there are situations in our lives that bring us to our limit. It seems like we have reached a situation like that. Prayer surely cannot hurt."

That night we pray together and say goodbye to Puschel. It is a strange atmosphere. I think that this farewell is very hard for Puschel, too. We know that a lot of her friends all over the world are praying for her today. In Sweden, the Torchbearers even set

---

[46] In the meantime (in Germany), you can see a TV feature film about the end of the GDR and the former president. It is called, "Honecker und der Pastor".

aside a room for two days that will be open for prayers for Puschel. Tomorrow, the day of her surgery, they want to pray for her all day. Nevertheless, it is hard for us to feel God's presence.

Eight Hours of Patience

The next time, we can take our time visiting Puschel. Eventually Myri and I meet up for a cup of coffee and prayer in the early afternoon. Any moment now we should receive word from the doctor about the outcome of the surgery. He promised to call my cell phone. It actually does take a solid eight hours before we receive word: "Everything went well. The surgery went as planned. But the sciatic nerve was enclosed by the tumor. It had to be cut and taken out with the tumor."

Puschel's right leg will never function properly again. Myriam is sitting across from me at the table and is watching me carefully while I talk to the doctor on the phone. After I hang up, I tell her what I was just told. I want to thank God for the surgery but it is not easy for me, even though everything went well. It *Puschel will be permanently disabled* doesn't get any easier as I call Eva-Maria right afterwards. She calmly says, "My Hannes, let's look ahead now." Yes, she always looks ahead and does what needs to be done. I am so grateful for her strength and that she trusts God as we do. When we are finally allowed to see Puschel in the ICU, she is thrilled to see us. But she wants to know too quickly what we know about how the surgery went.

Tears flood my eyes. I need some time to swallow the lump that forms in my throat. For now I have to tell our daughter that she will not be able to walk again very soon. She will always have a disability. Puschel, who has always had an athlete's heart and has always enjoyed running, asks with tears in her eyes, "I will never be able to run again?"

Helpless, I try to soften my answer. "Let's focus first on getting your energy back and getting you back on you feet." I can stir a little hope in her. More nerves could have been affected, including those controlling continence. They might be unaffected. The doctor cannot tell yet. The feeling of gratitude is mixed with disappointment that God did not do a "real" miracle after all.... I am supposed to be here to encourage my daughter.

However, I cannot really hide my disappointment anymore. Still, we pray together and thank God. There are enough reasons for that. At the same time we ask Him to continue to help Puschel. After all, she is His child, too, and not just ours. Puschel does not stop trusting Him. Tough weeks lay ahead. But she looks ahead, one step at a time.

Post-Surgery
Kidnapping in a Wheelchair

Puschel recovers astonishingly well from all the effects the surgery had on her body. She continues to live out Matthew 6:34: "Therefore do not worry about tomorrow, for tomorrow will worry about itself. Each day has enough trouble of its own" (NIV). It is an up and down period. Her meds need to be adjusted, and in only 14 days, the chemo rounds are supposed to start again. After only 10 days she is asked to walk with the help of some assistive devices. During those weeks, Eva-Maria and I have to alternate. We try to give the nurses a hand, and Puschel is grateful we don't leave her alone anymore.

Even Myri and Eva alternate coming to Berlin for a few days now and then. In the beginning of September, Eva-Maria is there again. It's especially hard for her when Puschel suffers. Both of them long for the day of Puschel's discharge to go home. By now, she has been in Berlin for four weeks already, longer than ever before. Puschel is still a real teaser, however.

The doctor looks into two teary eyes One of the residents, whom Puschel now knows a little, tags along for the next to last medical round. In front of all attending doctors, she asks him to remove a spider and its web from the window. He is nice enough to agree to it, but he doesn't realize that spider and web are on the outside of the window. So, he smacks the windowpane with his hand, and Puschel has a laugh....

The next day, September 15th, the last medical round is scheduled. Eva-Maria is standing next to Puschel's bed, as always, while the doctor talks to her. He tries to explain that, in his opinion, it is too early for her to leave the hospital. However, he felt it wouldn't be long now until she is discharged home. He pauses and looks into two teary eyes. Puschel no longer has any strength – she can only respond with tears. All those hospital stays have sapped her energy too often and for too long. Puschel remembers something her little brother Silas had jokingly told her once in the very beginning in Plau am See: "I will get you out of there – just holler!" She doesn't feel like joking anymore. She tells the doctor that her family has already gotten an alternating-pressure mattress which will allow them to gently transport her back home. Friends who own a medical technology business provided this mattress for her "on the fly" on Saturday. So, he didn't even have to worry about ambulance service.

The physician looks at her silently for a while. Finally, he sighs and says, "Okay, fine. I will prepare the discharge papers."

Eva-Maria sees the silent joy in Puschel's eyes, and she knows we must not disappoint her now. So, she calls home, and we start off for Berlin.

The following little message is posted to her website that day:

Dear friends, Puschel is allowed to come home today. Her younger brother, Silas, and I are leaving for Berlin now to pick her up. We are grateful that it is possible. Pray for a good and safe transport.

We meet up with my dad and his wife, Christine, in Berlin and drive to the hospital together. Dramatic scenes are unfolding in Puschel's hospital room when we get there. Eva-Maria had already tried to sit Puschel up on the edge of the bed yesterday. That did not go well at all. Puschel's new wheelchair is beside her bed now. Her discharge papers, together with the medical report, are just being handed over. Puschel is already sitting up on the edge of the bed, waiting for us to help her into her wheelchair. Suddenly, her eyes roll back. White as salt, she falls back onto her pillow, unconscious for seconds. Eva-Maria quickly puts her hand on Puschel's forehead – it is wet and cold. I am already on my way to get a doctor when Puschel opens her eyes. "What's wrong?" she asks, dazed. "Maybe we should get a doctor again…" I tell her. But as she lays on her bed completely powerless, she vigorously answers, "No way, we are trying it again." Aunt Christine gets a piece of corn sugar from her purse to help Puschel's circulatory system. Corn sugar always induces vomiting in her, and it is about to do so again. But Puschel swallows it determinedly. The words, "I want to go home at all costs," are written on her forehead.

We try sitting her up again, slower this time. Puschel is pale but she sits up. We lift her into her wheelchair. "Okay, now let's get out of here quickly," she says. Nobody is supposed to see Puschel's ashen face. She quietly tells Silas, "Go ahead and get the elevator in the hallway so the door is already open when we get there." I tilt the wheelchair back to bring Puschel into a lying position. She can rest her head on my arms. Everybody else is packing up her things and we head toward the elevator as quickly and inconspicuously as possible. Along the way, another patient who likes to talk a lot wants to engage Puschel in conversation. Eva-Maria explains to her that, unfortunately, we do not have time right now. When we reach the car and lay Puschel onto the alternating-pressure mattress, a smile lightens up her face. She is going home.

That evening the website reads:

Thank you so much for your prayers. Yes, we experienced the faithfulness of our Lord once more today. The transport went well. Puschel is very glad to be home after so long and for the first time since her surgery. The bones in her pelvis will need time to fully grow together.

How is Puschel Supposed to get Back on Her Feet?

That is the big question now. First and foremost, she needs to be stable and get her pain under control. The next chemo is already coming up again. How can a body bear such major surgery plus so many chemotherapy rounds?

But there is no alternative.

The following months are shaped by the consequences of the surgery and by resuming chemo treatments. Despite the repetitive blows to her immune system, Puschel picks herself up again – slowly. There are no personal journal entries, no emails or phone calls to friends during this time. Her body and mind are too weak. It pains her a bit that she cannot write. It is not only beauty that she has to surrender to the other young ladies for a while, but also her strength and energy. Her fundamental vitality, however, does not leave her even now. By the end of the year, Puschel can move her right leg again. The remaining muscles seem to compensate for the missing ones.

Puschel Writes Again

Favorite Verse

P uschel is allowed to be home during Christmas and New Year. On January 10th she posts a letter for her friends – the first letter since her second surgery:

I would like to share a few thoughts with you now on one of my favorite verses in the Old Testament. My dad wrote down those thoughts when we talked about it, but I couldn't write myself.

Now I can share them with you. It is Isaiah 41:10: "So do not fear, for I am with you; do not be dismayed, for I am your God. I will strengthen you and help you; I will uphold you with my righteous right hand."

"Do not fear" – that is an assignment. It is more an order than a simple statement or promise. It is exactly what God wants from us. It is, if you will, a commandment; because if you are afraid, you belittle Me, the eternal God. That's why you shall not fear. The reason for "do not fear" lies in God and His presence. "For I am with you." It does not depend on the situation and how bad it is; it is He who counts. There is a song that says, "God is near; He is incomprehensibly near." That God is near is not just a promise but a statement of fact. That fact, in turn is not dependent on whether we accept or deny it. We can ignore it or wipe it away, but we could also accept it as a gift. God is with me. He doesn't force Himself on me. But if I so choose, I could have the greatest potential available – the big Creator God. It depends on the perspective of my life. I think about Peter here, too, standing before Jesus on the water, ready to walk over to Him. But he gets scared of the waves. Jesus, however, is near, even when everything is going haywire. And HE knows what's around the next corner!! "Do not be dismayed." He wants me to stand here as His child, giving testimony of His power: Look at what an almighty Father I've got! I am learning to be patient right now, to stay submitted, not to give way, but to fix my eyes on HIM. And you all so wonderfully help me with that through all of your prayers. That's how a deadly threat, including

serious cancer, loses its deadly scare. Because I am in His hand, and if He wants to, He will heal me. And if He does not want that, then I am going home to Him for eternity. That has been my actual strength these past months; and you help me so tremendously to make this strength consistently visible and effective in my life, my body – my mind – and sometimes even on the pictures. I thank God and all of you for that! I pray that all of you and all of us may have a very blessed and fulfilling year in 2008.

More and more people who do not know Puschel read her letters now. Puschel sees that as an opportunity to share her innermost thoughts with those people.

Maybe you wonder sometimes about the many happy and occasionally rather crazy pictures on my homepage. As a matter of fact, we are often quite jolly. It is a huge gift, and I view it as an answer to all of your prayers. I know that hard times may still lie ahead and will come; but whatever happens, I am still at peace with God's paths. There are days now, too, when I do not look as happy. Those days my dad is usually not quite as enthusiastic about taking pictures of me.... (Surprise, surprise! And who of you would like to see pictures of a Puschel when she's hit by nausea and pain anyway?) But it isn't always this way. Nevertheless, I am grateful for every day God bestows on us. And I delight in everyone who prays for me. However, all of you who are praying for me should also trust that God will hear your prayers. Our Heavenly Father is always with me, even when I am getting chemo treatments and am at the end of my rope physically.

As If My Life Started Over

As Puschel gains strength, she can also tentatively put weight on her right leg. But she is getting inflammations again, including on her feet. So the chemo is halted.

On Sunday, February 24th, 2008, she writes in her journal:

Many days have passed and many things have happened. This week the last scheduled chemo is supposed to start. It is unbelievable for me. Father, it is as if my "life" was started over. Despite everything, I cannot believe it. This past year was full of small and huge events. We laughed and cried a lot together, but we prayed even more. Father, You have taught us so much. Thank you for the time and the strength which came from You alone. The surgery went very well. God saved the nerves responsible for my continence. HE helped me accept that my sciatic nerve was severed and to train my remaining nerves/muscles,

A new independence – Puschel is extremely happy to be driving through nature for hours on the "Grizzly," just taking pictures and enjoying God's creation.

despite chemo. In the beginning, I thought about what it would be like to be pain free and have lots of energy again. Gradually the pain did lessen and I did regain my energy. The entire time God put people by my side who encouraged me. Over and over again, I heard how other people were and are blessed through my illness. How could I ever bring any charges against God? My beloved Father, I also want to thank You for the clear MRIs. May it stay that way. But Your will be done. Father, please bless the Bible reading times I've started to share with Judith and Maria. You want to hear everything from us and talk to us. It makes one marvel at God... how many great hours has God already given me ....

When the last chemo is over, Puschel can even take part in our Easter Sunday church service, which is a milestone in a time of so much back and forth. She arranges meetings with the young girls of our church congregation for joint Bible studies. It's getting better....

April 21st, 2008 – My dear friends, one year has passed since I had to leave the little tropical country in Central America, El Salvador, and come back to Germany. I call it the transition into the second period of my life. Never before have I been so obviously close to the edge between life and death. Yes, we can die at any time for so many different reasons. We are shown ahead of time only very rarely. "Thank you, Lord, that I may live. To You be the glory and honor!"

Many a time did I ask Him to take the pain away from me, but I also always added: Your will be done! When I couldn't really pray for myself anymore, you all helped. That, too, is a big grace for me. You've accompanied me so faithfully with your prayers that His peace never left me; not when I was facing the small and big surgery, nor during the time I was far away from reality in the "Nirvana of the chemotherapy...."

I was able to get to know HIS big family! A lot of things are different today than one year ago. And I thank God for everything He gave me through all of you, too.

In my family, a few things have also changed. All of us have experienced God so closely! We would never have chosen this way. But we have experienced that HIS ways are good. And I long for nothing more than for all of us, and all of you, to rediscover HIS faithfulness and realize that HE is waiting for us to trust Him. Thank you for everything. Thank you for your love, your prayers, your bearing with me and us. HE is here. I want to praise HIM all of my life!

I Love Life – Revival

May 7th, 2008 – Chapter 2 of my life is starting. Thank you, Father, for these days. Every day I get stronger, and You let me see the beauty of this world.... Help me, Lord, to rejoice in all of that. I want to honor YOU in everything. I want to be patient and continue to take one step at a time. Would You allow me to have a horse? Always grant me the one wish: to be really close to You! Eva and Julia are currently visiting. Let them see YOU in everything we do together. Thank you for Inge's and also Myri's visit during Easter. Would it be possible to go to Aidlingen during Pentecost? If not, I want to be patient.

This May, Puschel is clearly taking a turn for the better. It is questionable whether or not she can go to the annual Pentecost youth retreat in Aidlingen because of her fluctuating blood levels. But it works out after all. She manages the eight-hour drive really well and enjoys seeing so many of her friends in southern Germany again.

May 27th, 2008 – I am 25 years old now.... Thank you, Father, for all my wonderful friends, every single one of them, through whom You share Your love. Lord, I am nothing, and yet I am valuable to You. How come? I would love to spend my whole life just thinking about You or who You are. At the same time I want to do so much. I love the life You gave me. Help me to do the right thing and go down the path You prepared for me. First of all: thank you for this day! I was able to start it with a few new T-shirts and a new cell phone. And then... well? I went for a horseback ride with Cia.[47] I galloped by myself. Then I ate tortillas, and went to "Plassis"[48] and looked at pictures from a long time ago. After physical therapy, Judith came, then Bobbel, and later Titus with his family. Kai was with Silas anyway. Maria came later after everybody else left. Daniel delighted me with a call, and after that, Myri. The prayer group sang a song for me with the entire Zinser family. After talking to Eva on the phone, I watched a movie with Cia and Tanze.[49] I checked my emails and translated my homepage. That was it with all my lovely friends. Thank you!

Puschel is very encouraged seeing so many of her friends at the Pentecost Youth Retreat in Aidlingen again. Most of them she has not seen in years.

---

[47] Lucia, one of Puschel's childhood friends
[48] The Sunder-Plassmann family
[49] Konstanze, Lucia's sister

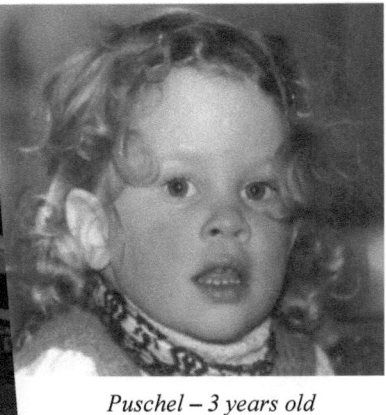

Puschel – 3 years old

Puschel with her big brother, Titus

The Holmer family – living in Bülow for two years now (1986)

Animals are her great passion

Puschel in El Salvador with visitors from Germany –
her "little" brother, Silas

With some of "her children"

"Her" little sweeties are loving her a lot

Puschel could always find joy in the little things,
especially God's creation

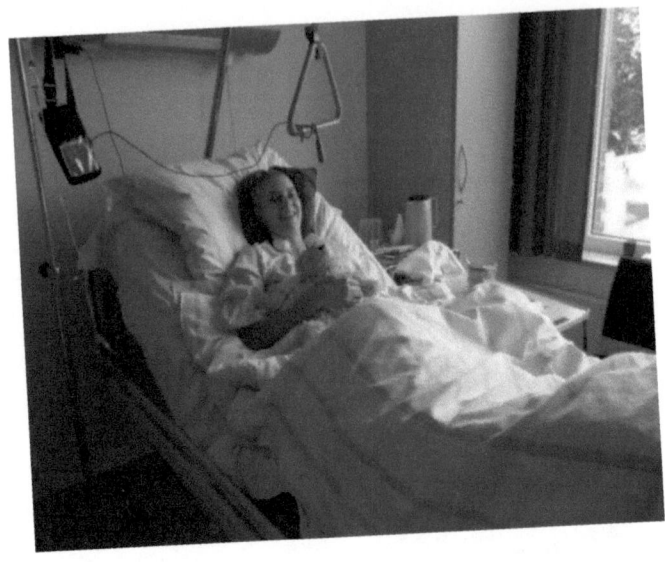

In all suffering, Puschel always had a lot of happiness

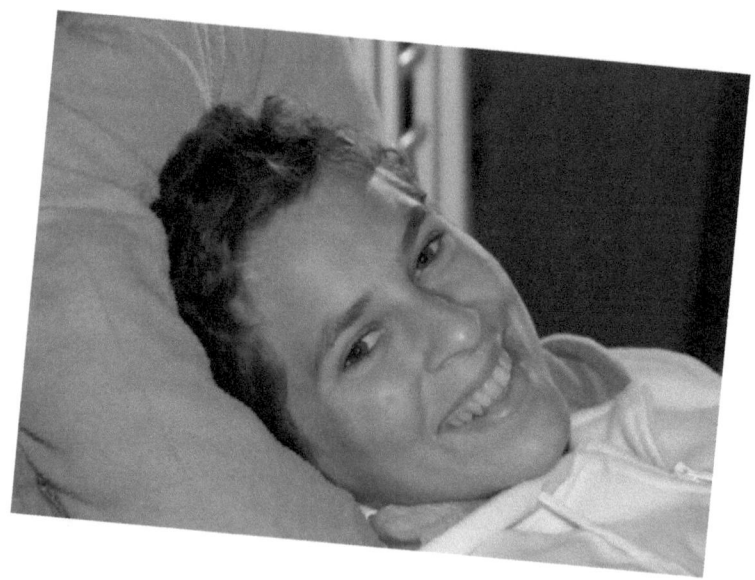

Puschel with her mother shortly before leaving for the hospital in Berlin

Puschel with her father shortly before leaving for the hospital in Berlin

... without a comment ....

Above: The good fortune of this world....
Below: Puschel and her grandfather

One of the best and most relaxed times on earth –
the journey to America

*Puschel could relax perfectly when painting her pictures —
and she passed on much joy in giving them away*

A Broken Fibula in the Pelvis

Almost one year after the big surgery, Puschel is suddenly in inexplicable pain. The doctors quickly find out the cause: the fibula that was put into the pelvis broke. The doctors call it a stress fracture caused by the chemotherapy, which prevents the growth of cells. During such beautiful summer days, this is very hard for Puschel, but even now she does not lose her cheerfulness. Who else can say that the fibula in their pelvis is broken? In her personal journals, there is no mention of this event. However, she is dealing with many periods of weakness, which keep her from journaling on a daily basis. When new examinations are scheduled, she writes:

June 18th, 2008 – Yesterday, I had to go in for examinations again. Another three months have passed. Lord, let the results be positive! But Your will be done! Lord, when I hear about the places people go for missions, I get butterflies in my stomach and would love to jump on the next airplane to get to know another country....

Wondrous Encounter with Lara

...I got a letter from a girl named Lara on my birthday. She is a granddaughter of a friend of Grandpa's who was a pastor

in Guestrow. She came across my website "by accident." After Pentecost, Myri got a letter from Anna (16), whose older sister Karin has terminal cancer. Myri wanted to give Anna (who, like her parents, is not a Christian) a book that was supposed to be picked up by a friend of Karin. When they met each other they found out that it was the same Lara who had sent me the letter. Confusing, isn't it? That was God's connection. He has a sense of humor. He loves to amaze us.

A friendship develops between Lara and Puschel, which lasts until the end of Puschel's life. Lara, who is very sick herself, is a "walking miracle" to Puschel. Puschel is excited beyond all measure when she finds out months later that Lara has met and later married a young man named Joe, despite her permanent illness. She is even more excited when she receives word that they are expecting.

Video Interview with Puschel

Little by little Puschel regains strength and can devote her time to new tasks:

Daniel asked me if I wanted to design the stage for the teen camp in Gaertringen[50] and video an interview. Lord, I need You! You instructed us to tell others about the things You do in our lives. Please help me then to do just that.

The videos for the teen camp in Gaertringen are taped indeed. A friend, Dominique Pfeiffer, who is the spiritual leader at a music camp here in Bülow, interviews Puschel in six parts. (You can find those interviews on YouTube under the heading "Lydia Holmer" or "Puschel Holmer" – channel, "Johannes Holmer.") The scenery and stage decoration exist to this day. It is always Puschel's biggest concern to let as many young people as possible know something about her joy with, trust in, and love for God. This is a great opportunity to do so. Eternity is real for her. It is the dimension that determines all aspects of her life.

---

[50] In southern Germany

June 24th, 2008 – Father, today I got the message that all my examinations went well. Oh, I am not sure how to thank You. The "what-if" question pops into my head sometimes. But that is exactly the thing I can surrender to You. Jesus, You know how I am. Help me, please, to be able to focus better during the day, so.... Oh, I want to live in Your presence with purpose, want to show You how much I love You, how grateful I am for Your mercy. How can I show the youth? I want them to see YOU— Jesus, Father, the Holy Spirit – when Maria and I lead youth group on Friday.

Most of our youth love to talk about Jesus with Puschel. There is great sincerity and openness when Puschel invites them for Bible reading times. A whole generation of youth is permanently shaped by it. Puschel's only wish is that they see Jesus and experience God's glory when they are with her. Maria, one of the youth who becomes a good friend (and is now the wife of Puschel's younger brother) writes:

In 2008 – Puschel started a girls' fellowship group. Back then I didn't even know what a fellowship group was, which is why it was just called Bible reading. I am not sure if it was Puschel's intention or if it just turned out that we were just a girls' group. She always prepared something for us and often we got two or three questions to ponder for homework. One Sunday I told Puschel that I wouldn't be able to come on Tuesday because I had biology class on Wednesday and a ton of homework to do for that. She just said, "Maria, God will give you back the time you spend for Him – often even more." What was I supposed to answer to that wise sentence?! On Monday in school, we were told that our biology teacher was sick, and the class would not be held on Wednesday. So basically, God gave me back the time in advance. This "time management" has accompanied me ever since, even though I had to remind myself of it often during my college days. Still, I have already shared Puschel's wonderful saying with many people. Time with God is most important!

August 17th, 2008 – My pen was missing, but this book didn't miss it. We had the grandchildren's camp and Fritz was here. Silas was at a seminar and has now left for Ethiopia and arrived

122

safely. But you can read some homesickness (from his emails).
We went to Sweden together and saw my beloved Holsby family
and, among others, saw "Joho" and his family again, too. It was
very nice, and I hope to see him here in Germany as well. Myri
is visiting right now with Luis, his sister, and mother. Myri and
Daniel have been dating for about a week now. Let them find
happiness with YOU! I haven't called El Salvador in a long time.
I hope everyone is well. Bless the people there and the work –
most of all, the children. Fill every corner of my heart, Jesus. My
life is Yours alone.

Annelie

Everyone who visits Puschel to just see her, comfort or encourage her, are in fact comforted, encouraged, and inspired by her. She loves to tell the kids at the summer retreat groups, which hold their camps on our church property, about her life.

August 28th, 2008 – Another group of kids was here today –
a camp held by Aunt Mary. I was allowed to tell them about You
and the things You do in my life. Let them see You when they
think back to this day (Matthew 5:14). Fill my thoughts every
day anew. Fill them with Your Spirit and Your love so my fellow
human beings may be saved!

Annelie is a young staff girl working at one of the kids´ camps. Sitting slightly apart from the group, she hangs onto Puschel's every word as though soaking it up. She stays in her spot after Puschel is finished talking and asks her a ton of questions. Puschel is delighted and keeps talking. After the camp days are over, Annelie seeks Puschel out once more, this time for a long conversation. Two days later we are going to drive to Sweden with some of our youth. Suddenly Puschel asks, "Shouldn't we ask Annelie if she might want to come along?"

"Sure, we can at least ask," I say. Annelie says yes – and later she wonders about that herself. After the trip, she often comes to Bülow for extended visits. She tells us about that time:

In the beginning I thought I was doing Puschel a favor by
spending a lot of time with "the poor, sick girl." It was vice

versa, because she connected me with the most important person in my life today. During that time, I was able to witness Puschel mastering everyday life with Jesus. I was part of the prayers, Bible readings, and conversations that reflected a trust and confidence in Jesus. Despite my initial hesitation, even doubts, I put my life into the hands of the Savior only a few months later. The words of the Bible were as normal here as food is part of everyday life. With everything I heard about the Father in heaven and witnessed in the everyday life of Puschel and her family, I discovered that the Bible is alive.

I saw that Puschel had the strength and courage to follow new and unusual paths because of her closeness to Jesus. Her gratefulness in every life circumstance impressed me the most. Often I didn't find anything to be grateful for. She did. She reminds me to this day to be grateful to the Lord for everything (Ephesians 5:20). Now I am especially grateful to have learned to see God, who has affected my life in His own way through Puschel.

No Fear of Contact

September 12th, 2008 – I got my first single-lens reflex camera, a Nikon D80.

September 16th, 2008 – It is the first time I am allowed to sleep somewhere else (at the Dehn's in Lobetal) while I am in the hospital. MRI and CAT scan results are already here. Father, I think in extreme situations, one is able to appreciate good things when everything previously in life has gone bad. And today I am filled with a deep, very deep gratitude. Jesus, we met so many nice people today. Many helped us out and were very friendly.

I realized today that I have regained a lot of my energy. Just like Alex wrote in an email: "…You do more than I, who is often too lazy." Sometimes one cannot appreciate it until one has lost all energy. Why do we sometimes lack the deep gratefulness for life? Does it have to be taken from us first in order for us to be able to appreciate it? So, I circle back to YOU in many important questions. You are A and O – Alpha and Omega! Let that be the truth in my everyday life also!

It depresses Puschel that most of the other patients she meets suffer silently and don't know that they are loved by God and can share their despair with Jesus. Every chance she gets, she talks to her fellow patients about Jesus. She has so little fear of contact that I am sometimes worried it could be a little much for her fellow patients. But it is not too much! People listen to Puschel, laugh with her, ask questions, and absorb God's love. They soak it up like a dry sponge from this cancer-scarred, but cheerful, young woman.

That summer Puschel becomes a godmother. Her little niece, Salome, is born and baptized. Puschel is excited and prays a lot for Salome. Late summer, 2008, she has another wish: she wants to attend the wedding of her Gaertringer friend, Steffi. That, however, involves a really long car trip. Added to that, she has another appointment in Berlin in the days prior. And with that, you never know....

The broken fibula in her pelvis has not yet healed. The examination in Berlin, however, proceeds more quickly than anticipated. She gets the green light to bear more weight on her right leg. We have a big car in which she can lie down comfortably. Thus, we take the drive to southern Germany. However, attending the wedding is not enough for Puschel. She also wants to give a special gift to the wedding couple. At home and during the entire drive, I have to rehearse a whole skit from the East German comedians, "Herricht and Preil," which we perform at the wedding together. That's Puschel!

September 22nd, 2008 – Two days have already passed since "JoJo's" and Steffi's wedding.... Tonight, I was allowed, to share about my life at the girls' fellowship meeting in Gaertringen. Father, I was not prepared for it, as so often is the case. Still it was probably exactly what the girls needed to hear. Thank you, Father, for Your help and faithfulness – not just this time, but also the many other times I have been able to talk to children here in Bülow. Slowly I am allowed to learn how to talk about You in public. Fill my heart with love always – with Your love, so it may reach my fellow human beings. Thank you for the wedding!

The church service was to Your glory. You were the focus. That was great. Let my dad enjoy his time here so he doesn't regret driving down here with me. Plant Your blessings into the next days with Eva, Maus, and "JoJo". May they be to Your glory! Thank you for my life. Thank you that I am allowed to still be alive.

Rehab in Sight

October 23rd, 2008 – Father, You know that rehabilitation is coming up. May it be a rehab for my relationship with You. I want to be excited for that time. During times of rest, I want to spend time with You – pray, read my Bible, draw, listen to music, and go for walks...all of that with You. Show me where to go. I long for You. May it become an "us" more and more. Is there room for somebody else? It shall be Your decision. Open doors and close others. Talk to me... I only want to go Your ways.

Bless the appointment at the unemployment office, too. Help me to reflect Your glory in the painting I am making for Sweden. Also, please help me to kick the morphine. Thank you for making the therapy possible so far. Thank you that my pain has been better. Praise the Lord, oh my soul, and all that is within me....

More and more often, Puschel is able to write emails again. She just doesn't want to lie around and do nothing but rather she wants to encourage others.

October 29th, 2008 – It is only by grace that I am still alive. When I look at pictures from 2007 I feel weak at the knees. Father, You pulled me out of a depth filled with joy and sorrow. Would it have been more merciful if I had died? I cannot answer that question. Lord, I need wisdom. "Show me, Lord, the way." We had a blessed Bible reading. Father, I am always in Your debt. We talked about sin. How we are all sinners. Even though it is incredibly hard for You to see our sin, You keep spending time with us. Lord, if You won't let something else or something better cross my path, then I will apply for rehab program in Füssen and will do a re-training for media design. Is that Your will?

It is (Almost Never) Everyday Life

December 11th, 2008 – Thank you for letting me see Your love for me through my parents, siblings, and friends. Thank you for my life here in Bülow all the way to El Salvador. Thank you for my childhood here on earth. I want to pass on that love by which I live to others. Donna asked if I could write a book about

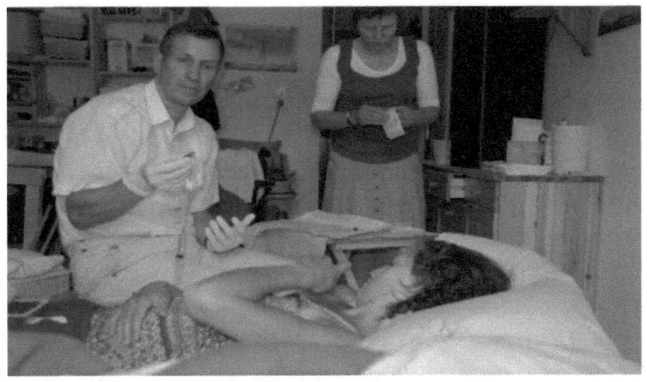

Laying needles for the port is always a joint task. First, we always pray. God has always granted success.

my life. Would You like me to do that? If I did, then only for You! Shall it be about gratitude? Something which will challenge readers to be grateful? Who should write it? Father, thank you for Mom. She works so hard every day. Bless her for it. Show me how I could take some load off her shoulders, and then give me the strength to do it. I love her; let her see that. Let Rebekka become a child of Yours, and everyone else in our youth group who is not one of Yours yet. Those who already follow You, may they develop a deep longing for You. I love You, Jesus.

December 15th, 2008 – It's been another three months again already. More examinations. We have to drive there again to-morrow. I wanted to write it down, but I was searching for my pen. I asked You and "Bubs" - here it was, in my backpack, vis-ible from my bed. Why does it always take me so long to ask You? Why not before everything starts falling apart? Father, don't let any more tumor cells grow, ever, if it is Your will. You made me. My life belongs to You.

Puschel is being examined in mid-December: X-rays, MRI, CAT scan, ENT, ECG, bloodwork. And all results are, amateurishly expressed, positive! In medical terms that is actually "negative" –

nothing (bad) was found. That means Puschel can start rehab. We got the message yesterday that insurance covers rehab as long as we pay most of the travel expenses ourselves. Of course, we will. Rehabilitation is going to be in Füssen, in a facility specializing in the musculoskeletal system.

December 31st, 2008 – You approved the rehab. I wish for it to be really a rehab for us both – to get to know You more! Oh, and what can I tell You about the results without any tumor cells...? What words would ever be enough to give You my thanks? Thank you, Father, for "healing" my body so quickly. I am laying down the problem with the pain! If it is Your will, take away the pain, or help me to endure it. Father, thank you for letting us find my new mattress when we searched for new kitchen chairs. Thank you that the money from the unemployment office was transferred that same day, too (so we were able to buy it). Thank you that my pain has decreased through it during the night. I want to praise You all my life. Thank you that I am Yours. Thank you for loving spending time with me. Myri and Daniel got engaged today. Bless their marriage. Thank you for "finding" a husband for Myri.

All friends and family who have internet access, appreciate being able to read about Puschel's health status on her homepage and they read all her letters to them. Many of them ask later if we can leave the page up permanently. We like doing that. All entries and letters can still be found there.

January 11th, 2009 – I received a presentation, rather a book from Myri. It is a printout of all the homepage pictures since April 2007, including all the letters I wrote for everyone. On one hand it seems so far away, on the other hand it seems very close. When I read the letters, I get goose bumps and tears. What huge gratefulness fills my heart!

January 28th, 2009 – Last week, I was able to go swimming twice. Walking without crutches (in the water) is so nice. Lord, do You think I will one day be able to walk without crutches? Father, may I use the rehab for that? I don't thank You enough for everything You have done and do for me. May I never lose sight of You! Fill all my thoughts day and night. What could be better than being in Your presence and doing Your will?

Rehab in Füssen

Will this rehab be revitalization for the two of us? Thank you for the time You will bestow on me. Thank you that I am already able to go horseback riding alone. Let the pain subside, so I can make the most of this rehab. If that is not Your will, help me to endure the pain.

The prayers for relief of pain are not answered this time either. But Puschel also prayed, "If it is not Your will, help me to endure it." And God does that. We do ask ourselves sometimes, however, why doesn't He take away all of her pain?

February 5th, 2009 – We are packing. My pain was so severe yesterday that I didn't know what would happen. I took some more Ibuprofen today and it is much more bearable despite all else. Thank you for hearing my prayers and those of many others. Thank you for Your mercy. Bless Grandpa's birthday party tomorrow. Bless all the conversations. Let them be to Your glory and bless others. I want to praise You! And then there is the visit to Bodensee which weighs heavy on my heart, Father. If You want, I will stand (and speak in front of the students) with the certainty that You will give me every word I need to speak. Make me serene, like an eagle in the air. And I put the rehab into Your hands. Show us what we need to pack; calm me and help me to stay positive. It shall be our time. A vacation together. You and me!

On February 8th, 2009 – Puschel is able to join the 80th birthday party of her grandfather in Serrahn. Three days ago SCM Haenssler published his book, "Uwe Holmer – The Man Who Took in Honecker". For Puschel, however, rehab takes the priority.

February 11th, 2009 – Füssen! Thank you for the safe drive here and the companionship of Mom, Dad, Maria, and Maus and for the visit at Bodensee. For a few weeks, I have been in more pain, and in the past few days it has been even worse. I woke up twice tonight already and by four o'clock had taken 60 mg of morphine and 800 mg Ibu.[51] *It has only helped a little. Father, please help me to survive this week here. Show the doctors what's wrong. Grant them wisdom so the right therapy may be chosen. And then give me strength, joy, and Your peace. Also, please help me in dealing with my roommate. May whoever will be here see You. "I lift up my eyes to the mountains – where does my help come from? My help comes from the Lord, the Maker of heaven and earth."*[52]

---

[51] Ibuprofen
[52] Psalm 121:1-2 [NIV]

A Rehabilitation That is None

A Mistake with Consequences

At this point, we would like to recount something to help understand the hidden drama linked to the time in Füssen. In the days leading up to the rehabilitation, we are in Berlin to get extensive testing done (CAT scan, MRI, X-rays). Based on the test results, the physicians in Berlin conclude that Puschel can start a rehabilitation program without any concerns. All the numbers look good; everything the best that could be expected considering the circumstances. So, Puschel starts the rehabilitation program that is designed to help build up and strengthen her muscles and make her bones resilient again. We support her as best we can. We get a hotel near the rehab clinic so we can spend time together. Something no one knows yet, however, is that none of the doctors in Berlin saw a fracture in one area of her pelvic bone and a crack in another. Under those circumstances, a rehabilitation program never should have been allowed. Everyone is surprised by Puschel's immense pain. Nonetheless she pushes through and starts with rehab.

Puschel starts enthusiastically

> *February 18th, 2009 – Your grace alone is enough.... During the past few days – no, weeks – I have been rattled. How am I supposed to do this? I am sick! One can't concentrate when one is sick.... Those are all reasons to ask questions but not reasons to give up. Father, I want to learn anew who You are. Guide my thoughts. And in return I ask You to help me walk again – completely freely and correctly. Guide this rehabilitation program, from the pain caused by the exercises all the way to the conversations about You with other patients. Let them see You during our stay here. I have been here for over a week now. It feels like a lot longer. Thank you for the friendliness of all the staff. "My Jesus loves me certainly...."*

Nobody in Füssen notices the fractures either, which is the next mistake. They even take new images of her pelvis because they want to find the causes of the pain. But they, too, overlook the fractures. Puschel does not know that she is investing all her energy in vain and fighting a hopeless battle – with a broken pelvis the rehabilitation cannot help, despite all efforts. But Puschel is desperate to improve her muscle strength and build up her bones! Questions like, "Oh Lord, why this, too?" keep running through our minds as time goes on. We still don't understand where God´s plan lies behind all this, and probably won't know until we are in heaven ourselves. But Puschel trusts in God even after the rehab, and we learn to trust more and more together with her as well. The doctors criticize Puschel for taking so many painkillers. But looking back, we are grateful for always taking her pain seriously and never questioning her intake of medication.

February 21st, 2009 – My Father, I am so grateful that I am so well off. Thank you for Your love and the love of my family and friends. You deserve love much more than me. What does it mean that Jesus lives within me? Galatians 2:20 – I don't have to ask anymore whether He can do this or that, as if He were next to me. No, He is within me, and I can ask Him to do His will and His work in me and with me and through me. My body is His, my mind is His. I want to give Him the opportunity to do with my life whatever He thinks is right. And I believe that Christ has set us free. And so I want to enjoy my life!! With You in me, Jesus! Show me what that means. Father, save those two who are sitting at my table.

March 4th, 2009 – It's been four weeks today. I was told today that I will only be here for three more days, and then my dad can come and pick me up. We will see. Today I tried to do everything calmly despite my full schedule, and it went great. I know You have Your hands in this. I want Your peace to be visible in my life. I know that whatever happens, it is not happening without Your permission. You shall have full possession of my heart. Is there a picture You want me to paint in which I can express just that? Father, help me to visualize my love for nature! Sometimes it feels like I am sitting on something like a knob on the left, and my skin is partly numb there. Father, You command us over and over again, "Fear not." So I am giving these symptoms to You. My life is in Your hands. Please let it be something benign. But, Father, whatever it is, Your will be done. Jesus, please help me to live my life to the fullest instead of wasting it.

Puschel gets through the rehab program and is full of peace and hope to be able to walk better soon and have more strength for life.

Inner Strength

As we write this, we sometimes think we should have found her journals sooner so that we could have encouraged her more. On the other hand, we also read that God, whom she trusts unconditionally, has everything in His hands, helps her with every step, and gives her inner strength.

March 12th, 2009 – To live in peace and quiet does not seem to be in the German blood. Life here runs so fast that you never hear yourself breathe. When I lie down in bed at night, I take one breath and then I am asleep. Jesus, I am so grateful that I am able to sleep! Father, I love Your nature. I want to go back home... to go for walks with You – like in Sweden. But I know, "Your will be done." But Father, what is Your will? Will I live for a while longer, and is that okay?

Finally Home

On our way home, we stop at the Torchbearer center in Frie-drichshafen – Bodenseehof. Puschel is excited to see her friends. She is asked to tell the students about her life – in English, which she loves.

March 12th, 2009 – Thank you for spring. Thank you that I can be home tomorrow. I am so excited, thank you! Thank you for carrying me through this last month. Thank you for all the encounters and opportunities to testify about You. Thank you for Your help the night I told the students at Bodenseehof about You. You really blessed that time. (See Psalm 32).

Finally, we are home. Still, nobody knows that Puschel's pelvis is unstable, and that she needs to be a lot more careful. She is concerned about the increasing doses of pain medication she needs. A few days later we receive bad news:

March 23rd, 2009 – Fever combined with twitching nerves, and at the same time being told on the phone that a shadowing in the lung was detected, was a little much.... But Father, thank you that this morning was the last time the fever has flared up. Father, I have bones in my pelvis that make noise as soon as I move. But I want to put it into Your hands and ask You to heal my body if it is Your will, and only then. You know what's right. I want to trust in that. Thank you! I did not deserve this. You do this because You are my Father, right!? Thank you, my Father!

A Huge Disappointment

Noise in the pelvis, and pain. We want to know what is going on. We ask the doctor who came into our church that day, and who is now head of radiology, for another examination. The results show that the pelvic bones are fractured. He then looks at the images from before the rehab and realizes the bones were already fractured before the rehabilitation.

The whole treatment, all that effort through all that pain, was in fact harmful! A small bone fracture is enough for us healthy people to take us out of commission. Puschel, however, now has to deal with this extra strain. Even worse, she is told by her doctors to reduce her painkillers. She becomes quiet, withdraws into herself, retreats to her room and her journals. Eva-Maria and I knock on her door, talk to her for a while, and pray together. I struggle to find the right words. Puschel cannot hold back her tears any longer. We take all of our disappointment before God. He could have prevented this. Why didn't He? After we pray, Puschel leans back in her bed. Her eyes are still moist, but her expression is peaceful and calm. What she writes in her journal that night does not read like an accusation.

March 31st, 2009 – Today we found out that I have already had a fracture in my pelvis since the examinations in Berlin. We just weren't informed. That means the fracture is worse than it would have been if it had been treated right away. Father, from a human point of view, this is more than annoying, but You don't want us to accuse the doctors, do You? I beg You, please show us how You would handle this. It is almost unbelievable that so much is broken within my body. I don't know what Your plan is in all of this, but do help me to continuously hold on to You. You promised that in all things You work for the good of those who love You. I don't know where this will lead, but You've got a plan. Thank you for the peace You grant me daily. Thank you for Your faithfulness. I don't know how stable my pelvis will ever be again, but I do ask You to let it be enough to go horseback riding. Help me to be able to once again attend the youth retreat at Pentecost. And how about the the summer camps in Sweden, or visiting Alana?! What do You think? I know there are other important things and people, but I would love this. Please let Titus' and Gesine's baby be healthy at birth. Right now, I am sitting at ProChrist.[53] *Open the hearts of these people for You! Show them what they have in You.*

Despite all the setbacks, Puschel does not give up but instead sets new goals.

May 2nd, 2009 – Please free my body of tumor cells and let my pelvis heal. May I be part of a prayer retreat in Sweden in May? I would love that. I already give You thanks. I am in more pain today. Please help it to get better and keep the complications away. I would be so excited [to be at the youth retreat at Pentecost] to see all those people I love. Let Johann become a child of God. Bless Eva and her family. Thank you for carrying me all the way up to this day. Thank you that I have You in my life.

Insight and Confession

June 13th, 2009 – Father, I have so many thoughts in my head right now…. Help me to sort through them and not to miss anything. Jesus, I know You can heal my body and let me rise like a young eagle. Mmmmm…. Actually, dumb: I

---

[53] An event with music, lectures, and accompanying program where participants discuss questions of faith

keep waiting to know whether I will continue to live, but will I ever know? I should live my life to the fullest. The point when my life on this earth comes to a close and I can start getting excited for eternity, I will only know when you show it.
Jesus would You take away my pain? I have not enough concentration – for example, memorizing Bible verses. And if not, help me to do my best. I know the time of my death is set. To You, Jesus Christ, be praise and honor forever.

Her thoughts are now constantly filled with the desire to rest. Puschel loves sitting by the lake that borders our property. Here she has peace and quiet, here she is alone with her God – one reason why she loves being home so much.

June 2009 – The lake is calm. The ducks chatter, and every once in a while, you hear the bubbling of some fish. The sun shines beautifully upon the lake. It is peaceful. I am recovering from an infection right now. Thursday, not even a week ago, we were in Berlin. What a wonderful present! I could cry for joy. The shadows in my lung are gone! Thank you for Your mercy! I cannot say more. Thank you!

It is a constant up and down – attacks of fever, chemo treatments, blood transfusions. In between journal entries are a lot of those things. But we are grateful for every little headway and every new day. Then Puschel comes down with another high fever.

July 13th, 2009 – My Jesus, here I am in Berlin because of a fever that has been annoying me for the past two weeks. I was given antibiotics and the fever went down. The question now is what caused the fever. The lung? An abscess in my pelvis which would need to be removed surgically? Or even a new tumor? My Lord, I am so tired of being sick. I am tired of being in the hospital. The nurses are very friendly, for which I am grateful. The doctors, too, but that doesn't change anything. I don't want to be a seriously ill young girl anymore, as one nurse put it today....
I had a break, and Dad was here. Thank you, Jesus, for the encouragement. Thank you that he encouraged me, and through him You lifted me up! We watched "The Lord of the Rings" together. Something interesting was said in the movie: "You

cannot change or influence the destiny for which you have been chosen, but what you do with the time you have is up to you."
My Jesus, help me to be strong enough to make use of my time on earth so that as many people as possible may become Your children and grow in their faith through this time. Psalm 34:6: Jesus, my confidence, Jesus, my strength!

"Dad, Could You Come Here for a Minute?"

"Berlin is calling." Puschel has the phone sitting by her bed, because she has just finished talking to one of her friends. But she sees the far too familiar number from Berlin on the display. I accept the call for her. It is not good news. Tumor cells were found in her pelvis once again – Job's evil tidings.

The end of July, 2009 – My Jesus, You have allowed it. Many asked You for the opposite. But You have allowed things to happen differently. I don't know why yet, and I might never know. I do not have the right either. Despite yesterday's news of new tumor cells in my pelvis, yesterday, I am incredibly peaceful in my heart. It is like sitting by the lake at sunset, and not one single wave creates a stir. That is the peace You promised me – just as a gift, undeserved. Thank you!

And It Starts Again...

July 31st, 2009 – The chemo hasn't started yet. I am sitting at the table this morning. I feel tired, but overall I am strong and would love to go on a trip. Thank you for the friendliness of the nurses at the hospital. Help us to get along with the doctors also. Thank you, my Lord, for your peace. Let joy grow from it. "Be still and know that I am God!"[54] The chemo is about to start now. How weak will I get from it? My Lord, You can let this miracle happen and give me the strength for Sweden and the wedding (Myri's). You can also make it so that I can go to the wedding with my own hair. If not, it shall not be difficult for me. Thank you, Jesus, for never leaving my side.

---

[54] Psalm 46:10

In Berlin, Puschel forms new connections with other patients again and loves sharing the reason for her cheerfulness. "Dad, would you drive over to *McDonalds* again...?" she asks every time with a grin on her face when she craves a burger or chicken nuggets. They seem to have certain flavor enhancers, which are quite the opposite from the hospital food. Before I take off, she quickly asks her roommate if she wants anything. "Dad is going there anyway...." And I am happy to be able to do something nice for my mostly cheerful daughter. Time goes more quickly for both of us this way. Often, we have several hours of break, so we drive into the city to visit Puschel's friends – Markus Spieker (at ARD[55]) or Thorsten Alsleben[56] (at ZDF[57]) – or to go for a little shopping spree. Never before have I visited so many clothing stores, which also of course have melodious names. We buy a laptop together that Puschel carries with her everywhere from here on out. This way she can watch movies, write emails, or even track her own internet page. More important for her, however, are the people she meets.

August 2009 – Jesus, I would never have thought that I could tolerate the chemo so well. Other than being tired, I do not feel anything yet. The third treatment is coming tomorrow. A heart-felt thanks to You. You have given me so much joy in so many small and big things during the past few days. From a hat to a MacBook – and encounters that had Your handwriting all over them. Pursue those people until they are your children. My roommate, Ms. K., and Linda also. Become visible and known to them. Awaken Julia's interest more and more also....

In between rounds, Puschel is even able to take part in a youth camp in Sweden. While there, her blood levels go crazy as a result of her last chemo. That was not ruled out but certainly not expected so quickly. Ordinarily, the blood levels should have dropped after our return home. Puschel is not deterred. She loves being in Sweden and sees it as a welcome/unwelcome change to see Swedish hospitals from the inside. With a wink, she comments on the blood

---

[55] German TV channel
[56] The author of the article about La Casa. A friendship with him grew over the years.
[57] German TV channel

transfusion – "Now I am getting Swedish blood." In the fall, Puschel is even able to go to her friend Myri's wedding with Daniel, a mutual friend from Aidlinger days. (In the past, Puschel would have really liked to get to know him better herself).

August 22nd, 2009 – "Be still and know that I am God."[58]
Yes, Jesus, I want to become quiet before You and know who You are. I am not yet doing my job very well here on earth as Your representative. I want to learn anew what it means to belong to You. Myri and Daniel got married today. I am happy that they have found each other. Bless their marriage – for them and all the people around them. Jesus, will I ever know that happiness and be allowed to have such a friend and husband by my side? Jesus, I want to be happy regardless of whether I have a partner or not, and simply through belonging to You! Let this fact slip into my heart and fill my heart with Your light.

Thank you for the encouraging conversations with some people here. Thank you that I have been able to use the port until now. Please help me and keep it from getting infected. Heal this spot. I ask You for a miracle! Keep me from getting a fever...!
Bless this night and the drive tomorrow.

Until Nothing is Possible Longer

Puschel gets more chemotherapy – until it's no longer possible. Until the chemo is pointless. Until the doctors in Berlin give up. They do not say that, of course. But the body does not tolerate any more chemo. Puschel and I are back in Berlin again and know that, from a medical point of view, it is a hopeless battle. Eva-Maria is being updated via phone. She encourages us two optimists even more. We do not want to give up. We know that God can! But does He want to? The oncologists in Berlin send us over to the radiologists. We know that this is only an attempt to comfort and appease us. They know that radiation will not do anything. But one female physician says, "I've heard something about a new form of radiation."

When we get to radiology, they say they want to use conventional radiation on Puschel. But that is out of the question for her. It

---

58 Psalm 46:10 NIV

139

would be a placebo anyway (a pseudo-medication that does not have any impact on the cancer). But we do not give up that easily. When we ask about heavy ion radiation, the doctor can't answer. But she does say, "Our head physician knows about this because he was helping build the ultramodern radiation center in Heidelberg until a few months ago." But she doesn't know what it is exactly.

We wait for the head physician. He explains everything patiently and clearly. It becomes apparent that if any radiation is useful at all, then this one would be: in an oversized particle accelerator, atomic particles (heavy ions) are fired at the cancer cell to kill it.

Relatively weak radiation rays that do not harm organs or tissue are fired from different angles and levels. They barely harm other tissue but hit the cancer cell directly and have a major impact there. That's enough for us to decide. The problem is that the facility is not open yet. It won't be until November.

The head physician promises to consult the colleagues in Heidelberg. He has a conference there in a few days anyway. "I will call you," he says, and we leave a little more hopeful. Puschel enjoys every single day. She can handle the pain medication well. We can exchange the port needles ourselves by now. We are a great team. Puschel keeps trying to make the best of her life.

September 5th, 2009 – I am sitting down at the dock. My cell phone can't catch even the slightest hint of the beauty I see from the dock. I can see the moon in the distance. Next to it are gently moving clouds.

Four geese flew over me with more grace than I have ever seen. A small moment. Shortly after, a big flock of little birds flew happily around in the wind. Many little spots in the evening sky. Thank you that You love me – me, Lydia Holmer – so much. May my love for You and the people around me grow even bigger than ever before.

I Can Walk Again – Without Crutches!

Puschel loves the meadows, the lakeshore, the expanse, and the freedom. She is a fighter and doesn't want to be dependent on the crutches anymore. So, for weeks she secretly practices walking without them. That's also why she is always at the lake. Then one day she hobbles over to us with her crutches and says, "Would you two come down to the pier with me? I want to show you something." On the way, she throws her crutches as far away as she can and just continues walking. She turns around, spreads her arms out, and says, "Well, what do you say now?"

September 14th, 2009 – Jesus, I can walk! I can walk without crutches! It might look a bit odd for people who don't know me, but that's how it is. Jesus, thank you for this joy. For about a week and a half I've been practicing walking down to the pier, and yesterday I showed Mom and Dad. What a joy. Thank you, Jesus!

However, the new (relapsed) tumor continues growing in her pelvis. For some time now, one can see and feel it from the outside. But at the moment, we can do nothing except wait. For Puschel, it is important that she reaches certain points and achieves goals that will further her progress and give her renewed enjoyment in life.

September 18th, 2009 – My Jesus, touch my body. Lord, chase away all the cancer cells. I want to live! Help me to take pleasure in every day, not to wait for goals to be reached and thus miss the day entirely. Help me to love every person the way You do. Jesus, do You think it would be good if I could have a little West Highland Terrier? I think it could help get me outside, even in bad weather. Open the door clearly if it is Your will!

A Little Dog, That Would Be It

Puschel's desire to have a dog isn't new, and it will accompany us for a while longer. Sure, Puschel loves animals more than anything. She already has donkeys, bunnies, chinchillas, and lambs. Now she wants to add a dog. But more and more, even we consider it as something important for her. Only a very small dog would be possible, however. Puschel thus goes on a hunt for several months for a small, suitable dog. Already at the beginning of her cancer, after her surgery in 2007, Silas and I managed to get her a quad bike (a sort of motorcycle with four wheels), to help her navigate the meadows and forests again without having to use her legs.

October 13th, 2009 – The day before yesterday, I rode the quad toward Tessenow and took a bunch of pictures. But a lot of thoughts and feelings swirled around in my head, and I really just wanted to talk to Jesus. At first I wasn't able to form a prayer. I didn't know exactly what to say. Deep down I asked Jesus for a confirmation of His work, even though I knew that He is there and holds the reins. When I was almost back to Bülow, I saw the beginning of a beautiful sunset. After taking a few pictures, I turned around and saw extremely dark clouds behind me, and nearby, golden rays of sun hit the fields. An unusual and peculiar atmosphere. And then a rainbow formed. I called Dad so he could also take pictures. The rainbow intensified. An unbelievable, full, even double, rainbow! Soon it was gone. Dad told me later that he had never before seen such an intense and colorful rainbow. Your faithfulness was visible in full splendor! Just when I was out there! Not before nor after. Thank you, Jesus, for Your assurance and Your faithfulness. Remind me of those colors when I become uncertain! Thank you for showing me Your beauty and love in Your own ways! Thank you for joy! Give me wisdom to do the things that bring joy to my heart. You want joy for my life. Show it to me. Grant me open eyes and ears so I won't miss it. Teach me to stay in conversation with You throughout the whole day. When I think about the colorful wild geese today, I can feel my love for You. Thank you!

His Plan is Good

October 19th, 2009 – It is becoming more and more apparent that doctors cannot do anything more for my health. But that is exactly where you, my doctor, get a lot of space to act. You have the power to heal me. I ask You, if it fits into Your plan – heal my body! Let the cancer cells disappear. Show me where to set my priorities so I use the time I have left meaningfully – for the salvation of those I do not know yet! My life shall be a song of praise to You!

Of course, we also pray together for healing daily. So do hundreds of friends. All of them wish for her physical healing. Puschel hears of people who are healed from cancer. Even though she has one of the worst diagnoses ever, she also has a Father in heaven who has the ultimate power! She is sure God wants to use her, and she wants to let Him use her. "No matter what He has in his mind, His plan is good!" she keeps repeating.

Before we receive word from the radiologist regarding the therapy, Puschel is able to visit Sweden once more.

October 29th, 2009 – Thank you, Jesus, for allowing me to come to Holsby once more. I don't know when or whether I will be allowed to come here again. But I give thanks from the bottom of my heart for all the loved ones that I know here, was able to speak to, and who pray for me. It is an honor to receive Your love through them. Thank you for Your faithfulness as well as the faithfulness I receive through my brothers and sisters. Yesterday, for the third time, I was able to testify about my life with You. Thank you for reassuring me that You will do the right thing with it. I also want to say thanks that Jeremy is here this year.[59] Meeting a brother who has gone through something similar is very special for me. It feels like I have known him for a long time. Will you give me the chance to get to know him better? I am excited to see what the last few days will bring. To You be the honor!

Atomic Particles in Heidelberg

The chief radiologist in Berlin actually does call. His voice suggests bad news. "The physicians in Heidelberg do not want to risk it," he says. "The radiology center is designed for brain tumors. The kind of radiation Lydia needs is unprecedented; it's not even in a test phase. They have no experience with it."

I can sense that he wants to conclude our conversation; Puschel's case is closed for him. Still I try to pin him down and ask, "What exactly am I supposed to tell my daughter now? That we need to fly to Japan or the USA? That the risk for a patient who has nothing to lose, absolutely nothing, is too high?"

---

[59] A young man who had the same type of cancer, but on his leg, where it was easier to perform surgery.

He becomes very quiet and says: "Okay, I will broach the subject again. I have another conference there in a few days."

Puschel's case is closed for him

"Thank you for doing that. We do not want to leave anything untried." Sure enough, he calls me a few days later directly from Heidelberg. "Mr. Holmer, they are willing to try it. But you must come here in December so we can do a preparatory surgery. Do you want to do that?" Of course, we do! Many examinations are necessary for this preparatory surgery.[60] So now it is off to Heidelberg.

November 13th, 2009 – On November 10ᵗʰ, I had to go with Dad to Wetzlar where he had a meeting, and then we went right on to Heidelberg to meet with the doctors and discuss surgery and heavy ion therapy. I was waiting for Dad in the hotel in Wetzlar that night. When he came back, we went downstairs to have dinner. Three men from the meeting joined us at the table. An old man next to me overheard what we had planned for tomorrow. When we were done talking, he wanted to conclude with a prayer. I have never felt so peaceful in my life. He prayed: "Your thoughts are higher than our thoughts, Your paths higher than our paths. For as the heavens are higher than the earth, so are Your thoughts than ours. And those thoughts are thoughts of peace."[61] Humanly speaking, there are so many dangers with the next surgery. But every minute more that I spend with You, I become calmer. My Jesus, I still want to ask You to preserve my nerves. Guide the fingers, eyes, and minds of the doctors. And let them feel Your presence in the room. Thank you that You will be there. Thank you for Your thoughts of peace.

During this surgery they have to shift some very sensitive organs in order to minimize further risk. We are in Heidelberg for two weeks and can stay in Mutterstadt with friends. I take every day of leave from work at my disposal. There are often down times, during which we can meet up with friends or drive to Bodenseehof. As always, we try to make the best of things. At the beginning of the new year, we are supposed to return for the surgery; the radiation is

---

[60] In the preparatory surgery, those organs that are close to her pelvis are shifted so that they will be protected from the heavy ion radiation.

[61] Compare Isaiah 55:8-9

scheduled for February.

It is "Precise Insanity"

And then it starts: Puschel is being radiated by heavy ions. It is "precise insanity" as she lies in this facility on a cot specifically designed for her and is moved around a high-tech room by a robotic arm. I am allowed to be there as she is being prepared for it, and I can follow the actual radiation process on the computer screens in the monitoring room. It is gigantic. The radiation takes a few weeks altogether. In the meantime, Eva-Maria comes to Heidelberg to replace me, since I have responsibilities at home in our church community.

March 2010 – Jesus, if You allow me more years to live, I know that my life belongs to You and I want to be available to You. It is by Your grace that I can write in this book today. Thank you for this gift, for this day of my life. As long as we hold on to things that are so important to us, God cannot work in that area - like a boy who discovers a gift in a bottle, puts his hand in, and holds on to it.

He can only get something out of the bottle if he lets go of it. Otherwise, he cannot use his hand or the gift anymore – he cannot pull both out at the same time. "Whoever wants to save their life, will lose it...."[62] My Father, my life shall belong to You!

I do not want to hold on to it. I want to be grateful for all the

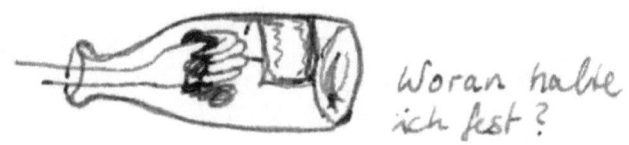

Woran halte ich fest?

"What do I hold on to?"

Puschel illustrated her own journal entry here. She drew and painted always and everywhere.

beautiful things You give me. But everything not so beautiful I want to accept in the knowledge that You will open Your eternal

---

[62] Matthew 16:25

145

kingdom for me one day and that my life here is nothing compared to what You will give me on that day. I have not deserved anything.

It is by Your grace that I am so well off. Forgive me if I think I deserve more. It is grace! I want to thank You. I often realize that in my mind I want to be healthy and live "normally," but I also realize that I am happy and peaceful inside. I am not missing out on the joy of life even though I am seriously ill. My tumor keeps growing and growing, yet I am not depressed. To the contrary. When I lie in bed at night, I sometimes feel as if I will burst with joy, just because You fill my life and are above it all. Preserve this joy in me!

March 24th, 2010 – A CAT scan was done yesterday. The doctor came by today (Thank you for my mom, who faithfully stays by my side). The doctor explained that the tumor has grown in size and changed in consistency – it's softer. I was not prepared for this. After I went for radiation again and took a nap, the world looked different again. Oddly, the doctor told us a few weeks ago that we should not panic if the tumor initially grows, because it could swell up. Today, however, she was the worried one.... Earlier I had tested the hardness. Now it is softer indeed. Well, it could all be positive in the end and mean that the tumor is being impacted and is shifting. Lord, heal the little boy we met today.[63]

March 28th, 2010 – "He gives strength to the weary...." (Isaiah 40:29). It is the Bible verse for today – I pleaded with You this morning to preserve my strength for walking and take away the tumor. You comforted me with Isaiah 40:31.[64] Thank you for not leaving me alone in all of this. Thank you for strengthening me again and again. I don't know what I would do without You. It is important to learn in good times not to walk alone, so that in difficult times we already know how to walk with You.

---

[63] She is talking about "Maxi". We get to see him again later on, and we form a very close relationship with his parents after Maxi's early passing at only eight years of age.

[64] But those who hope in the LORD will renew their strength. They will soar on wings like eagles; they will run and not grow weary, they will walk and not be faint. (Isaiah 40:31 NIV)

Jesus, will You help me to not see myself but rather the people around me? Especially to pray for them? Thank you that I have been able to live here in Mutterstadt with my beloved friends. Thank you that we were able to change the port needle without any complications. Keep infections from me and help me not need any MSI [65] *or the port any longer.*

April 4th, 2010 – The time of radiation here in Heidelberg is almost over. It went by more quickly than I first thought because of the infection and many other things. But it was long enough. I am so excited to get back to Bülow and into nature. Thank you, Lord, for places on this earth where I can see Your greatness in a special way. When I hear the birds in the morning, I also have to think back to my time in El Salvador. The hours in the morning we had together were special. According to the physicians, my tumor grew.

Whether it is swelling or actual growth has not yet been determined. But, Jesus, You know what is happening. If You want me to be with You, it will be for the best. But if You would like to use me to call other people to Your kingdom, then I also want to be content to do that. Grant me wisdom to use my life the way You intended. Let me be very close to You, in a close relationship without any compromises. I want to be purposeful and always count on Your presence.

A ("Very Ethical") Offer

The past months have been a very important time for Puschel. She has gained strength and health and experienced something one could call the "happy highlight" of her last five years. At the end of her stay in Heidelberg she gets a terrific offer.

April 10th, 2010 – Jesus, I do not know what to think. Arrange my thoughts. On Wednesday, we visited a Mrs. Dörges, who runs a charity. [66] *She offered to pay for a ticket so I could visit El Salvador once more. But what do You want? It would be wonderful to see the children again. But I do not know what You*

---

[65] Morphine sulfate by injection
[66] www.sabine-doerges-stiftung.de

want. I do not know whether I will live much longer. Jesus, I want to have used my time here on earth meaningfully. I need Your help for that. My tumor seems to keep growing. Jesus, watch over my body (without paraplegia). I want to walk...! You can do it!

April 21st, 2010 – Who would have thought that I could be back in Sweden this quickly again? John asked me this morning how I'm feeling in my heart. I haven't thought about that lately. Is it important? My heart screams for spending time with You. Take away the fatigue so I can concentrate on You more. Help me to overlook the pain and stop taking morphine through the port. Will You help me to use this week for that? It was interesting listening to George in the past few youth meetings and to talk about how people try to find contradictions in the Bible and how that blinds them.

Strength from Above

May 1st, 2010 – My Lord, thank you for Your mercy and for giving me strength for the past two weeks to be in Sweden and to have Eva and Judith here in Bülow. I don't take it for granted! Thank you that we were able to go to the Islaenderhof for horseback riding with Mommy yesterday, and that we made it back home safely. Grant me wisdom when we test a saddle next week. Let it be even better than I can imagine, so I can ride Saba again. Let me find suitable riding breeches also. You know about the offer to go back to El Salvador.

May 3rd, 2010 – Today I had the chance to walk down to the dock despite the rain and to spend quality time with Jesus. It was so good! I saw clearly again that He lives within me. I want to love You, Jesus!

May 4th, 2010 – I was able to go down to the dock again tonight. Thank you! I feel young like an eagle – as if I woke up anew. From a human point of view, I am deathly ill, but I don't even feel like I have a cold or anything. Today I read Psalm 30, in which David thanks God for healing – it was as if I had written it after I was told that I was healed. Will anyone tell me that one day? Oh Jesus, within me I have so much zest for life and joy! Preserve this joy for me! I love You and know that You mean well. You bless me tremendously. Don't turn my gaze from You. I never want to complain. No, Yours be the praise forever. "I want to dwell in the house of the Lord."[67]

May 6th, 2010 – My Jesus, I love You even more than three years ago. All this time You have been on a journey with me, which I never could have anticipated. You carried me through it, and I could be certain that You would not let me fall. What a Father, what a friend I have in You! You are the one who always helps me get up again and gives me strength when I don't have any anymore. You are the reason I am still alive, for many more people shall hear about You.

Jesus, I bow before You. I want to dedicate my life to You anew right now! You are the one who makes life worth living. There are so many people I have met at the hospital or elsewhere, and they are watching my life. I wish for one thing: that they realize You are the Lord, and they start believing in You. Nothing is impossible for You. That makes my life an even bigger adventure. When I look at a butterfly, I see that You are able to do incredible things. And if I look at the earth and everything that is upon and underneath it, I know that You are able to do anything!

Not Just Loving Father – Also Glorious Creator

Puschel still finds joy in nature around her home, in all shades of colors. It sustains her strength to live. The best time of the last three years has begun now.

June 4th, 2010 – What a gorgeous morning! I woke up first at 6 a.m. I can see the lake from my bed through some of the trees. The sunrays were only visible in some spots on the meadow. And to my amazement, a deer was standing at the edge

---

of the hillside. It was a heavenly picture. Shall I paint it? When I woke up again around 7 o'clock, the sun drew me outside. So, I walked to the lake after breakfast. To my annoyance, snakes were lying on the dock and did not budge. I am sitting in the paddock now, which is a rather snake-free area.... Saba is sunbathing about 5 meters away from me. The toads are making noises and the birds are chirping cheerfully. I can hear the workers in the fields and their machines in the distance, and Nico[68] is trying to steal something from me right now....

I am glad my two donkeys are well after they destroyed the stable together and ate all of the supplies of muesli and feed pellets.... I just injected my last MSI, and my port – that is my "plan".... Nico really just pulled away my backpack.... Jesus, You know whether I can stop with this amount of MSI or whether I have to reduce it even more. Make it work like this! Thank you that I've been able to use it during the last years. You know that it made many things a lot easier. Alana just popped into my head. Shall I try once more to get back in touch with her?

Not at the End of My Rope...

June 12th, 2010 – My Father, I want to go back to my first love. The passion is missing! If I am easy on myself, I cannot tell the young people that they need to be interested in You if they want to make the most of their lives. I don't want to be at the end of my rope, but I want instead to dedicate my life to You to the fullest, on the highest level – get all I can out of life!

"Don't be delighted by the success of your work for Me; the secret of joy is that you are truly connected with Me."

"Do you believe that I am able to do this?" (Matthew 9:28).

Do I know my Risen King? Do I know the power of His Spirit within me? Do I have unlimited trust in Jesus, who bursts through the limitations of nature?

---

[68] The donkey

This, too, illustrates her thoughts –
the drawing pertains to this journal entry above.

Every Day is a Gift

June 28th, 2010 – I am so well off! I am so well off! Yester-
day I was able to ride Saba on a tractor's path in the fields,
and later even do some dressage riding in walk and trot.

I was amazed at how easy it was. Jesus, thank you for this
time. It is like I am the eagle Isaiah talks about at the end of
chapter 40. I am regaining my strength little by little. Will I be
able to keep this up? It would be great, but I always want to be
able to say "yes" to Your paths, no matter where they lead me.
My thoughts are wandering toward the future. I want to see
whether You have different plans, or if You want me in Bülow all
summer and winter long. Time flies by so quickly. I don't want
to force anything, but I also want to live life to the fullest. What-
ever I do, I want to live life aware of Your presence. Would You
do that for me? I can't do it alone. Lead me by Your hand. I am
willing, but my flesh is weak. I let myself get caught up with un-
important things that steal my time. When I look into the trees…
Father, You are so… Hmmm, it is incredible to see the blaze of
colors! In the light of the sun, the bees buzz and the sky is blue….

Relationships

July 1st, 2010 – Jesus, I wonder how Lucia is doing. I miss her. This is probably what it really feels like to miss someone. I would also love to know how Alana is doing. Let us get back in touch. Please show me what I should write back to Sharon. Give me words that will encourage her.

July 2nd, 2010 – Thank you, Father, for this day. I have more and more encounters with people in our village, Bülow, and my prayer is for You to change these people here. Their hearts need You. Open them wide enough that they would all love to come to my wedding or funeral. Open doors for them, bless these people! Let them see what You can do. I pray to You, the Lord who has suffered for me! To You be the honor and glory. Hold on tight to my beloved youth girls, and Lucia as well. Maybe I can sleep on the trampoline tonight...?

We often go into nature like this. Puschel has her camera with her most of the time and just enjoys nature.

My Hope is...

July 23rd, 2010 – I feel a lot better today than the past few days. Thank you! This past night was finally restful. And now I am sitting on the bench outside. I can hear the birds chirping. Bees are humming. The sun is shining pleasantly warm. Yesterday was a special day –ladybugs, pictures of the sun and nature; and at the end of the day the smell, and especially the sound, of summer rain. And when I started praising God for the rain and saw that it is a sign of God's love for me, it rained harder – as

152

if Jesus wanted to make it clear that He has everything in abundance for me.

Thank you for this day today! It was a gift. I want to be very close to You. I am hungry to know Your wisdom, to know You. Help me! Father, my condition is critical from a human point of view. But from an eternal perspective, it isn't! I am at the end of this journey. Now it is important to make people aware of You... (Matthew 20:28). My hope is to live. My hope is to have joy in life. My hope is to find a spouse. My hope is to become independent. My hope is to make many people into disciples. My hope is to volunteer and help at an infant ward in Ecuador and to show Your love all over this world. My hope is to have a well-trained Westi or another dog for a friend. My hope is to one day live in a country where monkeys are at home and to give a home to a monkey. My hope is to bring joy and dreams to people through my paintings. My hope is to live at the beach. My hope is to canoe down a river and listen to the whispering song of the wind in the night. My hopes are of this world.

But they make no sense if You, my Jesus, are not in them. If You don't want to fulfill them, they will stay dreams. Only You know whether any of it (and if so, what) will come true. There is a time for everything. But I know for certain that You bless every little thing. The rain in the summer brings joy to people just because it sounds wonderful when it hits dry ground. You make the butterfly come alive to me simply by opening my eyes to its marvel. I delight in the laughter of a child because it is as if You are smiling at me. Jesus, my Redeemer, my Savior, my faithful Friend, my Bringer of peace and joy, who opens my ears and eyes and nose to the wonders of this world, fill my life like the laughter of a child receiving love. Open my senses to all that You do. Then I will learn what it means to live.

I do not want to be imprisoned in human walls anymore. Free me, so I will set my hope on You alone and nothing else. ONLY YOU SHALL BE MY HOPE! Nothing can be important if You are not most important to me. Fill me anew with Your fire and let it never die down!

August 2nd, 2010 – "You turned my mourning into dancing" (Psalm 30:11-12). This Psalm seems to be written for me or by me. The only thing is that I do not know how much longer I will live, and from a human point of view I am far from being healed.

But did the writer of the Psalm know that for certain? He wrote it anyway. Regardless, I got the diagnosis three years ago and yet I am still alive. Can't I thank you for that and sing a song of joy?

Back in Sweden, when doing the ropes courses, I always used the ropes as a metaphor with the young people telling them that they would not know that You keep Your promises until they let themselves fall.

Today I know – not just through a metaphor and from the Bible or from stories – that You keep Your promises. To be held by You is not a feeling of uncertainty – quite the contrary. You alone grant certainty. What a wonderful foundation!

Refueled with Strength and Joy

August 12th, 2010 – Thank you for the phone call from Mrs. Dörges. Thank you for her willingness to support me financially. Father, show me what to do with this. Grant me wisdom! Thank you for my condition. Let me become stronger and stronger. Do You think I will be able to go to Ecuador to help infants one day? Should I ask Mrs. Dörges to fund a Spanish class? Please grant me wisdom about how far I should help Titus and Gesine [69] concerning parenting, smoking... whether I have a purpose in that area. Thank you for Your love for those four!

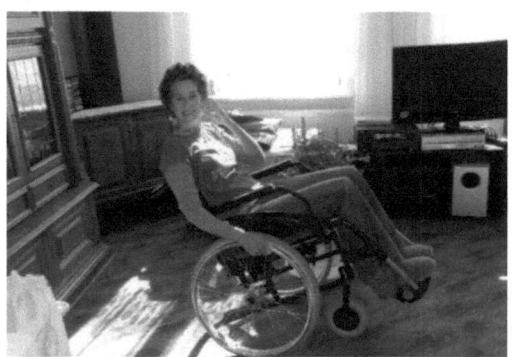

The sickness is everpresent — but that usually cannot diminish Puschel's joy of life.

---

[69] Puschel's brother and sister-in-law, the parents of her goddaughter, Salome

August 30th, 2010 – Helena's[70] baptism was yesterday. My Lord, bless her life and the people around her. She is a little sunshine already. Let her become even more so. I want to learn to expect miracles from You. You know how close I am to getting a little dog. If it is Your will, let it happen so I know that it is coming from You! Mrs. Dörges wants to fund a trip for me.
Where should I go? Where do You want me to be?

Thank You for Forgiving, Lord!

September 4th, 2010 – I learned something very important yesterday. I have spent the recent years judging people without intending to. But I did so by looking at their way of life and assuming they wouldn't include You, Jesus, in their lives. I pray that I only hurt a few. I put myself above them. That was wrong. In some areas, I am often no better. Father, in the daily Bible verse it clearly says again that You forgive us. I bow before You. Forgive my sins! I took a lot of guilt upon myself. Father, I really want to see my neighbors as You do. I want to love them as You love them. I want to forgive them, as You forgive me. I am ashamed. Father, show me, open my eyes to see what You want to tell me. Do You want to heal me? Show me whether it is right to fly out to Colorado this fall. And if so, with whom? Would it be good to go with "JoJo"?

September 9th, 2010 – Father, there are so many people for whom I would love to do something good. Help me to see what's important in Your eyes. Rearrange my thoughts anew. Thank you for the time with Linda! Show me where to go this fall. May I experience the fall in Colorado? The season when leaves change colors? Direct my path! There are so many people who do not know about You. Use my life as a blessing to all those who are still lost. I know that even when I am with You in heaven, You will continue to testify about Yourself on earth. Even then You can still use my life, but I would be most grateful if You would grant me a few more years. Nevertheless, Your will be done. To You be the praise!

---

[70] Puschel's second niece

America,
Here I Come!

From Colorado to Texas

S eptember 22nd, 2010 – It's incredible reading the last journal entry as I look at today. I am sitting outside at Bodenseehof right now. I just saw three squirrels. That makes my
heart so happy. How restful; how good You are for me! My diagnosis has faded into the background because I am feeling so
strong these days. During the past three weeks, I have gained a
lot of energy. I wake up in the morning and am not fatigued from
the night. Thank you! I can only say thanks. I feel like I cannot
do anything in return for You. So, I can "only" be happy.

The best and easiest weeks that Puschel lived to see within the
last four years begin now. She actually does receive a trip as a present. Mrs. Dörges, who founded the Sabine-Dörges-Stiftung after
her own daughter Sabine died of cancer, makes it very simple and
transfers the money to Puschel without hesitation. She tells her on
the phone, "If you are well enough to go now, go! Nobody knows
what will happen tomorrow and whether it will still be possible."

"We are in the process of booking a flight for Dad and me.
You have organized everything so fantastically. There is still
some stuff that needs to be done, but I trust in You. I love You,
Jesus. It is as if You have given me new wings. Like the dawn.
You are giving me back life. I don't know for how long, but I do
know that it is a gift.
I know that if things went in the opposite direction again, I
would still be in Your will. It would be easy for You to cause the
tumor cells to vanish, but You have Your reasons, good reasons.
I can rest in that no matter how much the storm rages. Let Lara
realize that again, too. Thank you that she is doing so well during her exams right now. I am just amazed and praise You.

Within a week, we prepare everything for the trip. We have to apply for a new passport for Puschel because hers expired. That works out well via express order – mailed in Mecklenburg and picked up at Bodenseehof! And indeed, we take off a few days later, flying into Denver, Colorado. We stay a few days in Colorado Springs with Puschel's friend, Kirsten, and then we drive to the Torchbearer Center in Estes Park, right at the edge of Colorado National Park, and meet Mrs. Thomas. She is the wife of the recently deceased W. Ian Thomas ("Major Thomas") who founded Torchbearers.

We visit the National Park with its unusual mountain peaks, look down upon green meadows and clear rivers, and stand by quiet mountain lakes that reflect the dark firs and grey mountains. We can even go for a walk in the Rockies with Puschel's friend, Lindsey – the girl she baptized years ago in a forest lake in Sweden. After the radiation treatments in Heidelberg, Puschel is strong enough to walk around in the Rockies without her crutches. Every once in a while, she holds on to my shoulder to keep her balance while we walk. After everything she has been through, it is a tremendous gift that she can move around so well on this trip. It would be fine with us if it stayed that way.

We rent a car and drive north. The destination is Moyie Springs, Idaho – right on the Canadian border. We pass through the Teton Range and Yellowstone National Park, then further through Wyoming and Montana, all the way north to visit Liesl and her family. It is an incredible trip which could fill a whole book in itself. During our last week, we return the rental car and fly all the way south to Texas, visiting Annelie (from church community) at the Torchbearer Bible School there. During this time Puschel reunites with a lot of her friends whom she met in Sweden.

Monday, October 25th, 2010 – Wow, I am looking back on three weeks in the USA. You blessed that time exceedingly. To You be the praise. Thank you for every single day. Thank you for the strength. Oh, how much I give thanks for all the beloved friends I was able to see again. More than I planned for myself, You kept track of everything. David and Melinda emailed me and said how sorry they were to be on the same continent but not in the same city with me – not knowing that they were driving to Idaho at just the same time we were!

When I finally was able to see Lindsey and her family again, she asked if I was meeting Daniel in Idaho as well, since he would surely like to see me .... So, that happened, too. I want to see my beloved brother again after so many years, being able to spend magnificent time together. Father You know how much I would like to see him again. It is in Your hands. Bless my brother. Help him to keep his gaze fixed on You. It was amazing to see that my beloved friends love and know You even more.... Thank you. You are the one who enriches their lives. I could write so much about the past three weeks. I am hoping to print out the pictures of the beauty of Your nature – Your creation!

Reset for the Future

I have a lot on my mind now. People I love and people who need to get to know You better. But first and foremost, I want to start reading Your Word again daily and spend quality time with You. You have given me strength again to read Your Word. Talk to me, I want to listen! Grant me wisdom to correctly train my dog, which I hope to pick up at the end of November and who will be a friend here in Bülow. Also, please bless the young people, and show me what my job is here. I could jump with joy.... I do so in my heart because I have You – and that is my greatest gift!

I Will Not Die of Cancer

November 1st, 2010 – "King Jotham grew powerful because he walked steadfastly before the Lord his God." (2 Chronicles 27:6) Peace. Yes, that's what You grant everyone who trusts in You. I have been pretty exhausted the past few days, and I am a little apprehensive about getting bad news from Berlin on the 18th. I asked You, Father, what Your plan was – whether You will let me die from the osteosarcoma after all. But in the end I will die because it is God's will and not because of the illness.

I have now opened a different book in my Bible – John, and chapter 11. I quickly got to the verse 4 which was underlined. It says that Lazarus won't die, but that his sickness is for the glory of Jesus and His Father. I told Jesus that I still don't know if that is true for me also.

158

November 24th, 2010 – You have definitely changed my heart. Weeks and months ago I was longing to share my life with You, Jesus, on a daily basis. More than a year ago, I realized that the devil had stolen my zest for life. I asked You to give it back to me. However, it is hard for You to hand me something when I don't even stand before You to communicate with You. How stupid of me!

You can be free on crutches, too – here at the Baltic Sea

Even Annoying Things Are From Him

The point is to thank Jesus, because no matter what He allows to happen, He allows it for certain reasons. And those reasons come from His goodwill. The point is to thank Jesus for even a missed ferry because He also has His reasons for that. Ever since last Wednesday and the days prior to that, Jesus has made me more sensitive. When something happens that seems annoying, troublesome, or even hopeless, HE wants to hear that we still trust in HIM. He wants us to thank Him for bringing us to the point where we trust in Him, hand Him our anger and hatred and anything else. Since then, I have been in conversation with Him. What would it have mattered to be healed physically but not to have any of these experiences and thus be sick in spirit? Humanly speaking, this might be weird but, Jesus, I am glad You have brought me this far. I don't think my heart has ever been this content. Father, now I am asking You for the fire, the will to tell people about You and to be courageous. Grant me patience to bear the things I cannot change.... About two weeks ago I did not have any strength. I told You that I really wanted to go to Sweden again but needed strength for that. Since Wednesday I have not been quite as tired. I am on my way to Sweden now because You granted me strength for more than just one afternoon.

With Heavenly Strength to Sweden

It is heaven-sent energy, as well as Puschel's determination to go to Sweden again. (How many more times?) She wants to celebrate Thanksgiving with friends there. I cannot go with her this time, and Eva-Maria is not confident enough to do so. But Puschel demonstrates her persistence. She asks me to take her to the ferry in Rostock and asks a friend in Malmö to pick her up from the ferry in Trelleborg. Of course, it is possible...! That is Puschel. It will be her last visit there. Her friend, Rebekka, is one of the main reasons why she is so persistent and wants to go to Sweden so badly. Rebekka writes about those days:

In November of 2010 – I went to Holsby just for a few days to spend some alone time with God in the beauty of the area. Since I love snow, I had already asked God before and during my drive to Sweden to send snow. When I woke up that first morning in one of the guest rooms, I could hardly believe my eyes! It had snowed so much overnight that everything was covered in powder-white snow! Elke, the housemother, knocked on my door and told me, In the evenings, *full of excitement, "You won't believe this! Puschel is coming! All by herself!" I had told Puschel before my trip that I would come to Holsby for a few days. She had told me she couldn't come because she had not been feeling well. So to find out that she was on her way here was a huge delight. She came here all by herself for the first time, without a wheelchair or any traveling companion. She*

160

was given a room in the same house, which meant we could spend a lot of time together.

In the evenings, we often sat together in the little living room with a cup of tea and just talked. Puschel's dry sense of humor and her way of telling stories often made me laugh so hard that my belly ached. Her happy and buoyant nature often let one forget the condition she was in. For me, it felt like time had stopped. Outside, the snow covered everything and transformed the Swedish countryside into a dream world. Inside, we enjoyed a Swedish wood cabin, the creaking plank flooring, and the smell of a fire. And I was sitting in a comfy chair, all wrapped up in a blanket with a cup of tea in my hands, laughing. Across from me Puschel's eyes were filled with love, hope, and faith. The woman I saw was at peace with herself and with God. She was full – to the fullest. She could give, love, and be free as if she had nothing to lose. She was able to express truths so simply that they went right into one's heart. She knew everything was well because her Father in heaven was good.

December 1st, 2010 – The trip is already over. But Father, You have blessed every day so much. It was a special trip. The reality of my illness was further away than it has been in a long time. At the same time, it was more present for everybody than usual. Father, You really encouraged me through my brothers and sisters. Thank you for every encounter. It is so encouraging to see that there are so many young people who want to be led by You. Make them Your missionaries. Use them so that many more people will know You, will be grateful in the little things, and know that You mean well for Your children. You showed me that You can only reveal Your glory to us when we do exactly that. Gratitude and trust open the little window to Your greatness and glory. It comes more naturally to me to talk to You now. I do not have to make myself stay in touch with You. Father, please help me to not take Your work in me for granted. I want to dive deeper into the depth of Your greatness and be patient in listening to You and learn to hear Your voice.

December 5th, 2010 – It was a very blessed time, Father. Thank you for it! Rebekka was a blessing to me. We were able to spend quality time with You, and we understand each other. That was something very special! The students want to learn about You, which was encouraging to see. The guest lecturer was there with his wife. They are missionaries in Italy. They, too, enriched the week a lot. I was able to be there for Thanksgiving. Once again, I was able to see how much, and how much better, You plan! My meds lasted for exactly that time. I am back home now. I love You and am grateful to know You. Also, bless Daniel in Seattle. Show him who he is through You. Shape him. Thank you for him!

Joy

A Book That Blesses

*D*ecember 5th, 2010 – It is the end of the year; the new one hasn't yet started. But I think for me a new phase has started. Wow! When I read the verse below just now, I saw all that this word contains: "I guide you in the way of wisdom and lead you along straight paths." (Proverbs 4:11, NIRV) You lead Your children in small steps, not just in big ones. I take these words for myself, for here and now. They belong in my new phase. You dwell in me and are "ringing the bell." Father, I don't even need to ask You to bless this journal, for You are already doing that.

Oh, I praise You. Father, forgive me for making You so small in my life and making myself so important. What am I in comparison with You? People who write that my faith is a model for them have no idea that there is pride in me, and that I often fail to trust You. It isn't possible that my little faith can be an example to others – there's something wrong with that. Father, I am very serious. Abraham's faith – I want to learn to trust You with that kind of faith. It always has amazing results. Jesus, I am much richer today than I was four years ago. I can't understand anything nor can I do anything unless You give me the strength for it. Thank you that for months now I have no longer been carrying a burden. You are right: "My burden is light." You carry me. Jesus, I want to learn to expect the fulfillment of Your promises. Take me by the hand. I want to give You the honor.

Joy That the World Cannot Give

December 13th, 2010 – "How majestic is Your name...." These words started the morning and are still present at the end of the day. That's what I am feeling. Wow. I am not worth it... and You make me worthy. Father, I am more grateful than I have ever been. I feel like a baby who is just beginning to blurrily see its daddy. But to know that my Father takes care of me! He has *taken care of me. I come from Him. And I will go to Him. Father, I cannot imagine it yet, but how wonderful that I can walk. One day I will be able to walk perfectly. I look at this verse on the side: "For physical training is of some value, but godliness has value for all things, holding promise for both the present life and the life to come." (1.Timothy 4:8) It is crystal clear that it is more important to lead people to You and keep my eyes fixed on You than to focus on my body and my talents. Father, I am giving You my future. Take it for Your glory. You know the desires of my heart and what I really need. Thank you for Your little and big surprises. Like tonight, the post card from Donna which I had forgotten to open.... You provide! My Jesus cares for me. Why or what should I fear?*

December 14th, 2010 – I know, it is only grace – by grace I have been able to trust You so far. Father, I beseech You: Today I realized that I can no longer stand on my toes on my "healthy" foot. I need Your help not to give up. To You be the honor. Thank you that not even my foot can keep me from honoring You, Father! Thank you for the promise of comforting me and going with me through this valley of darkness. What would I do without You? Amazing grace. Father, thank you for letting me see Your work throughout the day.

It is the end of the best year yet. Puschel's condition has improved after the radiation in Heidelberg. The tumor has completely regressed. Instead of a bump on her pelvis, an indentation is now visible. However, on the inside, the cancer has not stopped spreading. Furthermore, there are spots on her lung that are still considered metastases. Puschel is gradually experiencing neurological problems again. Apparently, her nerves are constantly being "annoyed" by fluids or some kind of growth that is not visible.

They All Need You!

But Puschel does not just focus on herself and her sickness. Instead, she tries to focus more on the people around her – for example, the older women of Bülow. She visits them, drinks tea with them, talks and laughs. The women always delight in Puschel's visits and look forward to them. During Advent, she invites them for some Advent arts and crafts. And the ladies come.

December 16th, 2010 – Father, I have half an hour before the ladies of Bülow are coming, and I have to start preparing the room for that. Order my thoughts, Lord. Grant me peace. Let this afternoon be one of life's blessings for these beloved ones. Let them see You at least a little bit, so they start asking about You. Do not let them leave this earth before they have gotten to know You and Your love. Without You, my Lord, this evening is not important. Help me! Thank you. I want to keep my gaze fixed on You. Accomplish Your work, my Lord and Father!

December 24th, 2010 – Thank you for the time with You this morning. Abba, show me how to live my life. It makes no sense unless Your power in life, in my life, is visible. For there are so many people who have to see You in order to believe. Thank you for my certainty that You live. Thank you for Your joy within me. For patience. For zest for life. For the energy to keep living. Thank you for coming into this world and becoming a tiny human being. I want this humility to be evident in my life. Is it? I wrote to Daniel yesterday. I told him what I have been praying ever since Sweden, since I sat on that rock and saw the different sized trees.... Jesus, I want to be a tree that is rooted so deeply that it can also stand firm in storms. I realized yesterday that You answered my prayers: so far I am standing. Let my roots keep growing!

If This Is My Last Christmas

December 30th, 2010 – This Christmas was something very special. But Father, if it was the last one here on earth, then I want to thank You for making it so special. I also ask You for a special start to the New Year. Puschel is being prepared *Thank you, Papa, for the past year and a trusting gaze toward the future, where I want to consciously live out every moment. I want to fill my time with Your thoughts and only do the things that bring You honor – everything in the knowledge that I was forgiven for my "imperfection." That is grace! What a future!?*

No, it is not the last Christmas for Puschel. However, it is the beginning of the last full year. But Puschel is being prepared by God more and more. We do not really notice this, but her journals reveal it to us in retrospect. She does not talk to us about it that much. Our focus lies on daily necessities and treatment options.

January 6th, 2011 – Jesus, so much is happening. The New Year seems to have started a long time ago, but it has only been six days. Help me to sort my thoughts. You showed me so many things yesterday, but I am not even sure if I can remember it all correctly to start working on those things.

January 9th, 2011 – Today, at 3 o'clock, little baby girl Pia Julie was born. What does she look like? What may become of her little life? Oh my Jesus, become her number one! May she grow up to honor You and lead countless people to You.

January 15th, 2011 – My heart is heavy when I feel my foot becoming weaker and weaker. I know that every time I have gotten to such a point, You have showed me something! Thank you that You have not forgotten about me. Thank you! I want to continue to trust in You. You have warned me in many different ways that there would be challenges. Fixing my eyes on Jesus! Be Thou my vision…!

…And If It Means to Leave It All!

January 23rd, 2011 – My fountain pen is working again. What great joy, Jesus! Now I am going to write down my prayer for today. Knowing You is the best and biggest thing that could ever happen to a human being! Romans 8:21[71] is the verse of the month for February. Oh Jesus, I want to live in a way You would call life. What does that mean? Let me learn to love Your Word. It is my greatest gain to talk to You. Father, I do not want to pray, go to church, or read my Bible anymore out of duty! No, I

---

[71] …that the creation itself will be liberated from its bondage to decay and brought into the freedom and glory of the children of God.

want my heart to be on fire to love Your Word in a way I do not know yet. I never want to stop talking to You, because that is the best for me. Jesus, I just want to live life with You. And if that means I will have to leave my beloved friends – and especially my family – then I also know it is for the best. I want to be able to honestly say from now on that You are my greatest love.

February 3rd, 2011 – Titus survived the accident[72] and he looks remarkably well. He smiles more than usual, which makes me so happy. Jesus, grant me wisdom to recognize the different "love languages" of my family, and teach me to use them. You said that we Christians would be recognized by our good deeds. Change my heart so people can see You through Your power which is at work within me. I want to love every human being for the very reason that You made that person, which is the second most important commandment. And at the same time, my biggest desire is to love You. I am ashamed because I often do the opposite – I don't show You my love but instead break Your heart over and over again. And still You don't forsake me.

Jesus,
I Cannot Stand Myself

These days, we are out and about once more trying to find treatment options that might even still be out there. Puschel has not lost her optimism, although she realizes more and more that her condition is continually getting worse. She is one of the most patient and grateful people we know. But even she is under emotional pressure every now and then. Most of the time we do not notice it, but sometimes it shows.

At times, Eva-Maria has to go back and forth two or three times to get just the right food. Often, she has to go all the way to the attic to fetch Puschel's favorite clothes. She can alienate her mother sometimes by saying things like, "No, I will only take this injection from Dad." From our perspective, we do not take this so seriously. We see her constant pain; this is little in comparison. But she has always been so sensitive. Therefore, she does perceive such

---

[72] Puschel's older brother had a fire accident with serious burns to his face.

behavior that way. But we do not take offense at all.

February 18th, 2011 – Oh man, I cannot stand myself when I get all grumpy because of my fatigue or whatever. Most of the time Mom has to put up with it. I am so grateful for my mom! Thank you! What a blessing it is to have a place for rest and recovery at home. So far, I have always needed the rest after the hospital stays. The past two days flew by me just like that. First, the appointment at the Charité with a pediatric oncologist, and then the examinations in Berlin-Buch. We are supposed to get a call today regarding the results. We have probably reached the point where I have to decide if I want a new round of chemotherapy. That could make me start feeling sick again. Jesus, I need "the hem of Your garment." It seems You are the only one who can still make a difference. Somehow, I do not realize it yet or something. I do not feel like crying. My heart is at peace. My hope is bigger than ever before. Thank you, my Father. You want me to be Your servant. Show me how. Today Gesine[73] came with the kiddos. Bless my family, Lord!

To Live in Gratitude

It is around this time that we start to realize that, humanly speaking, we've exhausted our possibilities. However, we still try to arrange anything that might help. Puschel fights like a lioness for life and health. At the same time, she is firmly rooted in eternity. This rootedness and her prayers (and those of hundreds of friends who pray for her daily) have made her a person who has not had to ask for thankfulness for a long time....

February 21st, 2011 – Jesus, I want to live in thankfulness and not just talk about it. Help me with that! Last week the physicians in Berlin told me that they do not have any more therapy for me. But they do not know that I have the best "therapist." Jesus, don't do it for me (even though I want to live). Do it for the doctors and everyone who is watching me. I am saved for eternity, but there are so many who aren't. Give me a lifestyle of

---

[73] Puschel's sister in-law

gratitude in my heart. Help me not to cling to earthly things, not even to my life. Because one day I will see even bigger and better things.... I want to share exactly that with people and not keep it to myself. Help me to grow. Let us grow together so that nobody who knows me could doubt You are right here, and that there is no one who compares with You. Jesus, however long I might live, get whatever possible out of my life, so that people may see You and live to see for themselves who You really are. It wouldn't be fair if they didn't have a chance – I do not deserve it any more than they. And I want to live as Martin Luther once put it: "If I knew that the world was to end tomorrow, I would plant an apple tree today." Thank you. "He will yet fill your mouth with laughter and your lips with shouts of joy." (Job 8:21 NIV). I want to enjoy my life to the fullest – to live! Since You are my Savior, let my mind be clear instead of always so tired. I'm almost falling asleep, even as I write.

My Goddaughter, Pia

Today I want to give thanks for my new little godchild, Pia. Thank you that I was able to meet her last week. Bless this new week with You also! Please, let the weather be awesome. Even though the sun is barely out yet, please let it shine this week!

February 25th, 2011, 0:16 o'clock – Myri just told me on the phone while we were saying our goodbyes,[74] that she will read the children's book "my children" in El Salvador (that one I illustrated to), and she will tell them all about me and my animals. Father, I love those children. I love seeing pictures of them. Will I ever be able to talk to them again? During the past few days, a bunch of people wrote to me saying that they were fighting alongside me. Am I fighting? How can I? Am I too weak-willed?

...But You Are My Hope!

---

[74] Myri and her husband, Daniel, are leaving for an internship in El Salvador at La Casa. Before they go, they are taking a cultural training class in Canada.

February 22nd, 2011 – Getting fresh air is a pleasure. I love Your nature, Father. You created it beautifully. My body seems to fall apart more and more, the pain seems to intensify, my concentration becomes worse... but the joy in You, the love, the certainty that it is the smartest decision to give You every day of my life, grows more and more. My Jesus, I seem to be in a cycle from which, humanly speaking, I cannot escape. But You give me hope. You have a reason for everything. Thank you. Moreover, You give me hope not to give up. Fixing your eyes on Jesus! It is lambkin time. If it is Your will, give me a lamb. You know if it would be good. "He only is my rock and my salvation: He is my defense; I shall not be moved! (Psalm 62:6 NIV). Look after my whole body. Free it! Eva could take unpaid leave from work in July. Do You think I will be fit enough to fly to Canada with her to visit Myri and her family? Can I get the little dog Grace in April? Is it Your will? Father, I want to do what You want. But that doesn't mean I am indifferent.

The Little Dog Grace

Puschel talked to Winnie, a dog breeder from Dresden, on the phone. Winnie promised to choose the most beautiful and most suitable puppy for her. Even though Puschel only knows Winnie from the phone calls, she trusts her and waits patiently. Out of a very specific litter, Winnie picks a particular puppy. Puschel had asked for a pup that was very light with a dark snout, but Grace is the opposite: black from top to bottom. "This might still change," Winnie explains when we stop in Dresden to pick up the dog on our way back from the south. Puschel is exuberantly happy as she holds the little puppy in her arms. She names her "Grace."

From that time on, this little black bundle, which only weights about a kilo and a half,[75] follows Puschel everywhere she goes. Since Grace doesn't shed, she is even allowed to sleep in Puschel's bed. And after a few weeks, she becomes lighter and lighter, until she is an almost completely white dog with a dark snout....

Even though Puschel loves and delights in Grace every single day, the puppy was barely mentioned in her last journal entries.

---

[75] 3+ pounds

Now we see that Puschel's last reserves are being used. Her pain, and the question of how to combat it, are increasingly at the fore-front.

The Biggest Miracle: I Am a New Person!

March 13th, 2011 – Through Your death on the cross, Jesus, You freed me! I didn't "just" escape hell, and I didn't "just" get a place in eternity. No, the biggest miracle and gift is that I am a new creation. We are back to a paradise relationship. I can stand before You because Your blood freed me. I am the "prod-igal son" who can have a feast with You. You don't take me in as "only" a servant again. No, I can call You Father because You are merciful. I have not done anything to deserve it, it is by Your grace alone that I was freed. Jesus, it is no longer I who lives, but You living within me. Show me in the next few days what a difference it makes to be freed from my sins and thereby a new creation. I want to live my life, my new life, and I don't want to hide it. Let people see that You live within me (Galatians 2:19-20). They shall see You so that they, too, will be free. You know what is needed for that to happen. I ask You for mercy for my fellow human beings. Thank you. And I will take Romans 8:28[76] with me this week. I will write it into my heart. Thank you for Your love!

My Dear Friends

March 18th, 2011 – Oh my Father, You granted a blessed day yesterday. Mareike came for a visit in the evening. We talked, cried, laughed.... Thank you, Jesus! I gave her an assign-ment – to focus on gratefulness this upcoming week. Jesus, show her that You are there. Give her an experience she will never forget, please! Bless my sister. Show her how valuable she is in Your eyes. It was awesome to see Mareike smile again. Let that

---

[76] "And we know that in all things God works for the good of those who love Him, who have been called according to His purpose."

be just the beginning for her as she becomes a young woman who is sunshine to her surroundings! I am soon going over to Mrs. Scheel. Be at work, Jesus!

The same day, Puschel writes another letter to her friends for her internet page. It is the last one. After that it is impossible. This letter is so key that we want to quote it almost entirely. It is still on the internet page[77] as are all the other ones. But this one is almost like a legacy.

It has been cited many times by preachers and printed by magazines (sometimes in excerpts). Puschel can only journal until May.

It is the last letter Unfortunately, her overall condition now grows steadily worse. That certainly does not mean that there are only sad times for her and us all now. But her concentration and sight, for example, cause her more and more problems.

March 18th, 2011 – My dear friends, it is really hard to explain – my body is losing more and more functions, but my heart is filled with hope. It is easier to understand with this month's verse of March: "Truly He is my rock and my salvation; He is my fortress, I will not be shaken." (Psalm 62:6 NIV). Until now one might have thought that I am hopeful because I am optimistic, and because I think medicine is so far advanced nowadays that it will help me.

Just yesterday, I was talking to an elderly lady. She said the most important thing was to never lose hope. But hope for what? Her answer was, "...that you will grow old."

But I entrusted my life to Jesus once, and thus I don't need to cling to it anymore. From a human point of view, I would be ignoring reality by doing that because I am terminally ill! My perspective, however, is that of a human being who knows that Jesus is present, here and now. He does miracles. But it is about a lot more than just keeping me on this planet.

I will pass away one day like every single one of us. But I do have the certainty that I will experience a "world" much more beautiful. Jesus embedded this hope within me without my assistance. Thank you, Jesus!

Having this hope living within me does not mean that I am

---

[77] www.puschel.holmer.info

spared the "decay" of my body or that it doesn't bother me. Just yesterday I screamed to You, Jesus, as I felt so sick, and my pain was hardly bearable. And You answered my prayer. It was as if I was carried through the night hours by You. You carry me; I only need to ask. Why does it often occur to me so late that I have Jesus in my heart, and He is just waiting for me to ask? It is not His nature to force Himself on us. It is easy to forget what is really important amidst the busyness of everyday life. Who can I always count on 100%? I usually try to count on myself first. But that is simply stupid of me! I count on and rest in Him way too little. That's my own fault, I'd say!

To trust in Jesus does not mean, however, that He will just vault us out of uncomfortable situations. No, He is with us in exactly that situation of life. And if necessary, He will "carry" us. In hindsight, we have one more experience: He is there! I got a post card from a friend a while back that read: "I am always there. From, God!"

I wish for You and for myself that we learn to lean on Jesus more day by day. Only then will we have hope which surpasses death. Let us not forget eternity! The Lord is my rock. I want to trust in Him and never be shaken (Psalm 62:6). Some people think my life is only filled with sadness now. That is not the case. To the contrary. I am allowed to learn to appreciate a lot of things even more. My heart is thankful and thus filled with peace.

A few weeks ago, the doctors in Berlin told me after a few more examinations that they advise against more chemotherapy. The tumor in my pelvis and the metastases in my lung went right on growing during my last chemo treatment. It is more important to treat my pain now, because that will not decrease.

The last few weeks were admittedly pretty tiring, since the tumor continues to spread throughout my pelvis. My legs accumulate fluid, which "bothers" my nerves! We have had a lot of doctor visits during the past weeks and were guided step by step. It was one appointment after another. And the great thing is that we got the appointments much faster than usual.

So, I can hopefully report soon that my pain has become more bearable.... "Fixing my eyes on Jesus" – those are the words that keep rolling through my head. It is always my decision what I focus on and lean on. So, I am grateful when I can spend some time with Jesus in the mornings, because my day takes on a different perspective through Him. And what I want is to fill my life *with purpose, meaning to make the best of it. For that I need Jesus every minute. I feel richly blessed.*

The Last Journal Entries

When Puschel cannot write any more entries for her homepage, we keep doing it for her so her friends stay updated on her condition. Puschel still focuses on what is "really important" – that is the people around her. It is one of the big miracles God performs, one of the answered prayers God grants, that Puschel does not lock herself up in deep mourning. We all sense that God carries us through this daily, because from a human point of view, it is now hopeless. We are very busy with doctor visits, examinations, and the daily medications. But we are (almost) always cheerful.

That is God's gift, and it is His miracle in it all. Even though we (and many other intercessors and friends) wish for a different progression, we see and feel God.

March 19th, 2011 – Markus Spieker is not coming today after all. But Geli is coming for lunch with "Jonny"[78] and "Ela." Let him see You today. Father, let him see that You are alive. Father, save him! Show me what I can do. Open doors for the Teen Prayer Congress in Neubrandenburg.[79] Give me strength and less pain. Father, I need Your help. Take my body into Your hands. Arrange for me to have a driver and for us to be able to take at least a few teens tomorrow. Georg is thinking about going to Sweden during spring. Guide him and eliminate anything that keeps him from doing what You think is right – what is right. Bless him and his whole family. Bring them always back to You. Thank you for yesterday. Bless Mareike's day today; meet her where she is at!

---

[78] A man who has cancer and doesn't know Jesus
[79] A prayer retreat for youth in which Puschel would like to participate

...Freer Than Ever Before

March 26th, 2011 – Father, somehow it appears to me as if I delight in life more every day, as if I am freer than ever before. It is as if a load fell off my shoulders ever since the doctors said they did not know what to do anymore to help me. Jesus, it sounds really weird, but I am glad that they have come to this point with their wisdom. Thank you that Mom and Dad also seem to be at peace that You will lead us in the right direction. Let them never lose that peace. Protect that peace for them because it would be harder than anything else if I knew that they only suffered. I know they will always have a remnant of fear, right? But fundamentally, Father, I thank you for taking care not only of me but also my family. "May the Lord bring You into an ever deeper understanding of the love of God and of the patience that comes from Christ." (2 Thessalonians 3:5). Yes, Lord, please!

During these days, Puschel gets a request from ERF Media.[80] They want to know whether she would be comfortable giving a full interview. On a drive back from Heidelberg, we stop in Wetzlar. Puschel is feeling pretty badly; she can barely keep herself up on

Puschel with Markus Spieker, a Christian TV-journalist, and her brother, Silas, at Spree River in Berlin – April 2011

---

[80] Evangelical broadcasting – www.erf.de

her feet. But when we get to the ERF studio she gets so much strength that she sits through a 40-minute interview without any interruptions.[81]

Now I Can Lean on You

I give You thanks for freedom, hope, and peace. Thank you that I have never had to put my hope in people. Now I can completely lean on You without having to worry about whether the chemotherapy makes sense or not. Thank you, too, for expediting many things during the past few weeks. I know You won't desert me. You are at work. You overwhelm me – I can only marvel! To You alone be honor and glory for all eternity!

May 13th, 2011 – So much has happened during the last weeks. That's why I have not had a chance to write a few sentences here. The many meetings make it almost impossible. And besides that, I almost always fall asleep. My left leg has started to swell up because of the tumor. So, I need more lymph drainage. Silke[82] has been coming for a few weeks now. Father, bless her. Don't let her go without seeing You first. I can't use my foot anymore now. Will I ever be able to walk through Your nature again? Only by Your power! Jesus, You are the only one who can still do something. Intervene!

May 24th, 2011 – Jesus, Friday is my birthday. I want it to be a birthday – it is just hard to get the lovely people, everyone I want, to be here. Help me to decide correctly.

Puschel does not just want to celebrate her birthday. She wants to invite friends and relatives who are elders in the church so that they will pray with and over her and anoint her once more as instructed in the New Testament (James 5). She asks her grandfather, Uncle Markus (a pastor in the neighboring church community), and his wife Elke. And she asks a friend, Sigurd Havemann, who has cancer himself and has been sitting by her bedside more and more often during the last months.

---

[81] You can still listen to the interview today on Puschel's website (as of July, 2013)
[82] Puschel's 23-year-old physiotherapist

May 26th, 2011 – We are meeting up May 27th in the morn-
ing. Grandfather has also confirmed that he is coming. Thank
you! I just realized now that Psalm 23 is my life. During the last
few days I have had many flashbacks to my life in Sweden and
El Salvador....

This is where Puschel's journal entries stop. From now on we
only have our own memories, notes, or whatever Puschel's friends
or we ourselves wrote on her internet page.

Pain, Pain, Pain

Puschel is more and more distressed over not being able to move
her foot anymore. The tumor (the second relapse) compresses
nerves and lymph regions, which is why she can no longer move
her leg. Due to the pressure, her sensation is also decreasing continuously. We are glad and thankful to our fam-
The tumor com- ily doctor who supplies us with every medi-
presses nerves cal necessity. That is a huge blessing to
Puschel. Dr. Herrmann thinks a lot about what can be done now for
Puschel and puts himself into her situation. He always makes sure
that she gets whatever medications she needs. He also allows us to
do a lot of medically necessary things ourselves. We lay the port
needles, attach IV bags, and prepare vein access points for blood
samplings. Since her pain is becoming more and more unbearable,
we are now taking Puschel to an anesthesiologist in Rostock on a
regular basis. There she gets injections directly into the nerves that
are being compressed by the tumor.

At the same time we call the radiation specialists in Heidelberg
and try to arrange for another heavy ion radiation. "You want more
radiation for Your daughter, even though the first round did not
achieve anything significant?" the doctor asks. "What makes You
think the first therapy did not make a difference?" I respond, startled. "It was extremely effective. You just never asked." But the
doctors want to get rid of us. Another heavy ion radiation is not
normally performed after one and a half years. But what is normal
with Puschel in the first place? From our first visit in Heidelberg,
we still know that we need to be persistent if we want to get

somewhere. So, I explain on the phone that we want radiation as a palliative measure, simply for pain relief. When I keep persisting, they finally agree. We still have the mattress from 2010; nothing should stand in the way of Puschel's radiation. So we drive down to Heidelberg once again during the summer, so that Puschel can be examined before the radiation and the tumor can be measured. That is not a problem for Puschel. The main goal is to decrease the pain. Puschel pushes through: the eight-hour drive, a night at a hotel in Heidelberg, MRI, CAT scan, all of which she doesn't mind because of the prospect of relief. By the end of August, all the exams are finished, and we are awaiting a phone call to set the appointment. First, the insurance also needs to agree to all of this. But they take their sweet time.

Heidelberg Once More

On August 30[th,] we update the internet page for friends and other people, letting them know that the radiation is set for September 6th. We hope to get all required approvals. We now need to find a little room or apartment in Heidelberg, or nearby, in which Puschel can stay (with one of us parents and, if possible, little Grace) for the four weeks of radiation. Our previous accommodation in Mutterstadt with Mr. and Mrs. Bodisko is no longer feasible, as the stairs in particular are a real obstacle. Puschel could stay at the hospital, but she does not want that under any circumstances. We now hope that the insurance company will agree to an off-site accommodation and cover all costs. So, we keep praying for the heavy ion radiation to happen and for it to bring crucial relief.

The Insurance Company Takes Its Time

The insurance company, however, is silent. We can only wait and hope. It is September 5th, one day before the appointment. The phone rings. I pick up immediately. The clinic in Heidelberg is calling. "The insurance company did not get in touch with us, Mr. Holmer," the lady from administration says. I am getting discouraged. But the lady keeps talking. "However, it doesn't matter what the insurance company says. We will do the radiation for Lydia, if need be, at the expense of the clinic."

Hallelujah! We book an apartment right in downtown Heidelberg, put the suitcases into the car, and start driving. For Puschel,
four difficult weeks lay ahead. She does not feel relief right away,
but she knows from last time that it takes a while. We try to make
as much as possible of our time together. Every now and then,
Puschel can go for a little stroll in her wheelchair from the apartment into the city. Our family doctor at home has supplied her with
all pain meds and additional prescriptions. Puschel is thankful for
the trust of this doctor and for his efforts to help relieve her pain.
Sometimes she prays, "Lord, repay our doctor and bless him in
Your own way."

I myself have to go back home in between because of a wedding
and a few other duties. So Eva-Maria stays by herself to take care
of Puschel and Grace. They take a cab to the clinic. Grace, who is
of course not allowed at the hospital, always does a little dance
whenever Puschel gets back from her radiation.

Now That As Well – Meningitis

Return – and No Break

But then the day is here when I am back in Heidelberg, and I am excited to pick up my two (sorry, three) girls. A fantastic camp bed is prepared for Puschel in the car again; she lies there like "the princess and the pea." In the afternoon, Esther (Puschel's younger sister), joins us from Bodenseehof to drive up north with us.

We want to take off right after the last radiation. Everything goes smoothly. We manage the roughly 850 kilometers,[83] driving into the night, and making frequent pit stops.

When we stop at the rest stop in Dessau-East shortly before midnight to use the bathroom and grab a quick bite to eat, Puschel complains about a worsening headache. She does not want to eat anything. Back in the car, Eva-Maria says, "Let's just hurry up and get home!" We still have more than two hundred and fifty kilometers[84] to drive.

Puschel's condition worsens. She is at the end of her rope. Eva-Maria and Esther sit with Puschel in the back, praying and hoping. I am driving as fast as I can and concentrating as much as possible. Eventually we make it home.

However, as we are helping Puschel to her bedroom, she staggers and collapses. The three of us lift her up and lay her onto her bed. "Do you want to drink something?" Eva-Maria asks.

But Puschel only moans in pain; she just wants to lay there and get rest. We stand helplessly by her bed; all we can do is pray and put her into God's care. Tomorrow we will decide what to do.

---

[83] 528 miles
[84] 155.3 miles

With Emergency Lights into the Hospital

However, the next morning Puschel does not wake up. We try to carefully awaken her because the time for her meds has long passed. Puschel does not respond. We realize that she is unconscious! What now? We fold our hands as we always do and pray, "Lord, show us what to do! We need You!" Only a few moments later, I am dialing 911. I explain what happened. "Someone will be there immediately", the person in charge says. About ten minutes pass, then a helicopter rattles over our roof, landing on the field in front of the house. An emergency physician runs crouching toward the house.

At the same time an ambulance arrives. The doctor examines Puschel, turns around to us, and says, "To the ER immediately!" The paramedics put Puschel into the ambulance; Eva-Maria goes with them. Puschel is taken to a nearby hospital. They are fully equipped for primary examinations there. The diagnosis is quickly confirmed: meningitis. It could hardly be more dangerous. And help could not have come any later.

All necessary steps are immediately arranged in the ICU. When I finally get there, Eva-Maria fills me in on Puschel's condition. "If she remains stable for the next few hours, she should make it." The head physician, however, clarifies that statement. "You should be aware that we might not know for two or three days whether your daughter will make it or not."

An Odyssey Begins

An odyssey begins for Puschel and for us. In our rural hospital they are not able to treat Puschel's pain and administer the amount of pain medication she needs. To treat the meningitis (and to avoid the risk of any drug interaction), all medications that Puschel has taken up to now are halted. Of course, we do not have a clue what will happen when Puschel awakens. We keep repeating the names and doses of her pain medications and plead for these doctors to contact her oncologists and pain therapists. However, they don't consult anyone.

Since Puschel's primary pain medication is morphine, they have

181

to put her through a drug withdrawal. This causes drastic effects after three days. The physicians respond frantically and administer an extremely strong opiate that is usually used for anesthetization during surgeries. But this opiate cannot be used over a long period of time.

Eva-Maria's sister, Christine, and my sister, Elisabeth, who are both registered nurses, come to help us care for our Puschel. Elisabeth is Puschel's godmother and travels up here from the south specifically for Puschel. They trade nightshifts with us. In the following days and nights, we all reach our limit. We sit by Puschel's bedside and try to reason with the physicians to get Puschel the necessary medication. We stay by her bed, unable to bear seeing Puschel suffer like that. She moans, cries, hallucinates, trembles. We see the end ahead of us. All her siblings have come to say goodbye to Puschel. We want so badly that she does not die here. The women urge me, the father, to take her home! She should not pass away here.

That night, I sit by her bed and wrestle with God. "Lord, she is Your beloved child. And You said You would hear and act when we ask You to. Now I am begging You, touch Puschel's *The siblings gather to say goodbye* body and let her find rest." Puschel finds rest for the night.… But after 10 days, we "apply the emergency brake," and I demand either a return transport home or an immediate transfer to a tumor facility. Finally, the management of the ICU gets things going and arranges for a transfer to Rostock.

It is a chaotic transfer. No doctor accompanies Puschel in the ambulance, making an organized handover at the Rostock hospital impossible. We are drained, furious, and sad. We simply function, attend to Puschel, talk to the doctors and nurses, and barely have time to think. Every minute of rest is haunted by the question, "Oh God, why are You doing this? She is Your child after all!" Even at the university hospital in Rostock, the physicians are hesitant at first to change Puschel's current meds over to an appropriate pain medication. We are desperate and ask ourselves in the morning how we are supposed to survive the day. Then the director of pain therapy, Dr. Siems, returns from vacation. And finally, there is relief for Puschel.

Puschel is not herself anymore Dr. Siems immediately changes Puschel's medication. The drug that is completely unsuitable for long-term use, and has been administered in absurdly high doses, is replaced by an adequate morphine-based drug.

He knows that Puschel now has to go through a second withdrawal. He barely leaves Puschel's bedside in his palliative care unit. He admirably supports Puschel and us during this transition, and the high transition dose of morphine can soon be reduced. It is a hard path for everyone. Puschel is not herself anymore. She has been under a kind of anesthesia for the past three weeks. Even though she does rsespond every now and then, she is like a complete stranger. Later on, she can barely remember anything from those three weeks. She seems to have short-term recall of the events of this time, but long-term, her mind has not recorded any of it. How good that is…!

Not Even Two More Days?

In October of 2011 – Dr. Siems yields to our plea – against the advice of all of his colleagues – to allow Puschel to come home as soon as possible. It is clear to him that Puschel's time is drawing to a close. The hospital colleagues are convinced that she will not survive more than two days at home…. When Puschel can finally come home, Dr. Siems accompanies the transfer personally, even though

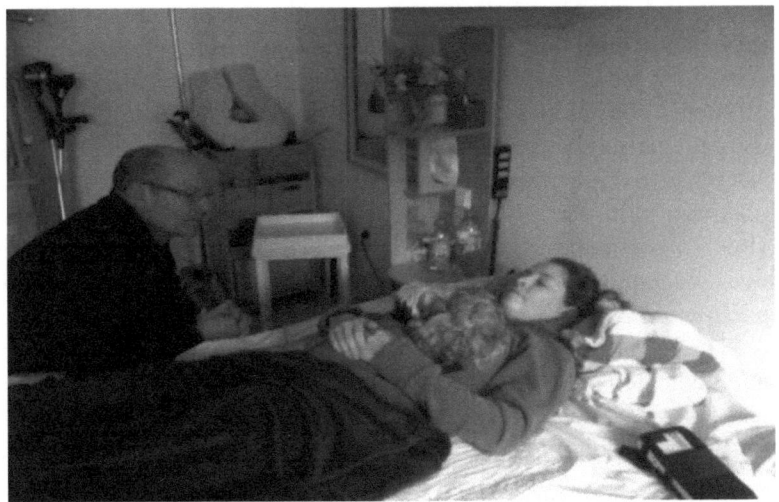

Dr. Siems comes to Bülow multiple times to look after Puschel.
We are profoundly thankful for his magnificent effort.

that is not his responsibility. We are sincerely thankful for his great efforts and also for the past weeks at the palliative care unit.

After four weeks in Heidelberg, 10 days at the country hospital, and two and half weeks in Rostock, Puschel is finally back home in Bülow on October 27th. Dr. Siems has wonderfully prepared everything for the transition home. And by this time, we are "experts" in this field and can take care of Puschel's medical needs almost entirely by ourselves. During the upcoming weeks our family doctor once more supplies everything necessary.

Christmas at Home

Puschel is still affected by the anesthetics, rarely awake, and hardly aware of what is happening. A few days later we get a sudden visitor: Markus Spieker from Berlin pops his head in the door. He just drove up here and wants to check up on her for a few minutes. I tell him right at the door that Puschel is pretty drowsy but ask him to follow me into her room.

When we walk into her room and I tell her, "Markus Spieker came from Berlin to visit you briefly," she opens her eyes and has a full conversation with him, which had not been possible till now. From that point on, over the following weeks, she is much more awake and clear-headed. So, even now there are positive signs and reasons for gratitude. And Puschel is always excited when Markus comes by for a visit in the following weeks. There are still many problems with pain and various other issues. The focus now is not the pain caused by the cancer as much as the aftermath of giving the wrong pain meds once the meningitis had subsided. There is some phantom pain, too, which is difficult to treat. There is neuralgia, which is difficult to locate. And there are multiple other symptoms that often appear for no obvious reason. It is possible that she is still experiencing withdrawal from the high-dose pain meds.

The upside is that all the doctors and nurses lend their friendly and dedicated support. We are thus able to handle most of the medical tasks ourselves, which is the best and most pleasant way for Puschel. Especially nice for her is that everyone who wants to visit her can now do so; this is much easier than *"Markus Spieker came from Berlin"* in any hospital. Puschel is clearly recovering in many respects. She is a lot more awake and can take part in the normal everyday life of family and home pretty actively.

As much as possible, we take her outside to get some fresh air or bring her to the table for family meals in her "lounger wheelchair." However, it is not certain which direction the gauge will go. If her body processes the many different meds well, there would also be a chance of a broader improvement once more. At the same time, it is completely unclear how the tumor has developed; we have no idea yet if and how the radiation in Heidelberg might have worked. We can only wait and keep taking it one day at a time. The most important thing for us is to have Puschel home again. We fight by her side, suffer, and laugh. There are even occasions of happiness again. We take advantage of those with thanks. Over the holidays we sit around her bed, pray, sing, and laugh with her.

Thankful for Every Hour Together

We understand that, from a human point of view, there is no chance of seeing Puschel in a healthier condition again. However, we are thankful for every hour spent together. Friends and relatives stop by continuously to encourage her. Puschel's cousins - Reinhild, Almut, and Magdalena - write:

When Puschel got sick and the three of us began moving back up north because of school or work, we started visiting Bülow

We always went home enriched

again more often. We wanted to help, be there, lend a hand (which got us the name, "the helping sisters"). We often realized that there was not much for us to do. But we were able to be there. One time we were just preparing dinner. We started setting the table on one end, while at the other end Uncle Hannes was busy preparing injections for Puschel. Since there was no doctor in the village, Uncle Hannes did the intravenous injections himself. Beforehand, he always prayed as one would before a meal – however, more as a request for a successful injection and for it to take effect positively. Even though we came to Bülow to give, we always went home enriched. In Puschel's presence, many a priority or a gloomy thought got set straight.

185

Some girls from our congregation come by with a keyboard, violins, and flutes to give her a little concert. Puschel loves that. A family from our church comes with the whole family for a visit; their daughter always came to Puschel's Bible reading for girls. After their visit, her mother tells us, "I was very preoccupied with my own thoughts, but as I left Puschel's bedroom, it felt like I was carrying an armful of presents. It was indescribable." Puschel's room is always filled with happiness and peace, never with sadness. Her cousins who live in the north now come by even more often. They enjoy being near her, want to comfort her – and are comforted themselves.

After one of those visits, Almut writes:

> *You taught me that I do not have the right to live my life however I please; that I am not entitled to be healthy or have a husband and kids or all the good things I do have. But I am to rejoice in everything I do have – a job and an apartment and food and friends, a family that loves me, and people whom I love. Sun and wind and clouds and sea and fields and rain and seagulls and mud and bicycles. Thank you for teaching me gratitude. Thank you for teaching me the way of forgiveness and for pulling me out of my victim mentality.*

An Unforgettable Walk

By the end of January, it becomes apparent that the kidney and other bodily functions are starting to decline. Suddenly, breathing becomes hard. Puschel has water in her lungs. The heart is slowly weakening and cannot eliminate the water anymore. Dr. Siems comes from Rostock to do a pneumocentesis (lung puncture) to remove the water. Given the circumstances, he does a fantastic job. We are incredibly grateful to the doctor for this (last) service, because it enables Puschel to breathe normally again.

It is January 31st. During these last days many come to visit Puschel again. Grandpa Holmer also visits once more. And of course, as always when he comes, there is singing and praying! Somehow everyody senses that it could be the last time.

In the late afternoon, Puschel's Aunt "Mary" (Maria) and her daughter, Hanna, come for a visit. When I ask Puschel whether she would like to go for a walk to the lake, she answers firmly, "Yes!" She likes to get fresh air on every possible, and impossible, occasion.

I lay her down in her wheelchair as usual. She still has enough strength in her arms to wrap them around my neck, so I only have to lift her body with one arm while I support myself against the bed with the other. Eva-Maria bundles her up, and off we go. It turns out to be a wonderful walk. The gray winter sky stretches above us, the frozen lake is calm, we see our own breath in the cold, fresh air. We push Puschel in her "lounger wheelchair" to the shore and carefully step onto the ice. On our way back, Puschel even jokes and laughs. Then she lies back in her bed again, grateful and tired. "Thank you" are her weak but clear words. Hanna can talk to her for a while and also read the Bible with her, too.

She writes about that last encounter with her cousin:

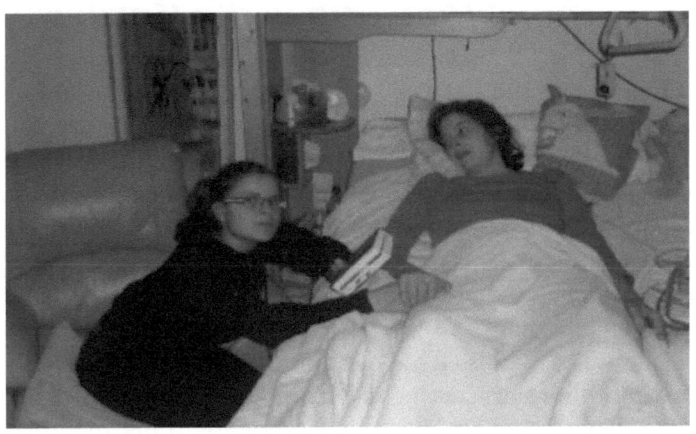

It is the last conversation that Puschel has in this world.

...then I remembered a verse that Donna sent me. I was supposed to read it to Puschel, which I had not done yet. What a "coincidence" that I remembered it right then. So I shared, "Peace I leave with you; my peace I give you. I do not give to you as the world gives. Do not let your hearts be troubled and do not be afraid." (John 14:27 NIV).

When I was done, I looked up and saw Puschel smiling. She just said, "That is a real good one." After that, she asked me to repeat it many times. When we had to say goodbye, she simply

187

said, "Hanna, I love you. You are a truly a special person." I was reluctant and only said, "Puschel, you can't be serious. YOU are a wonderful, very special person. You are a huge role model for all of your cousins because you show us how to be content with what we have. You show us that we can trust in God whatever happens, that He will guide us through, and He has it all in His hands. Thank you for that." Smiling and crying, she managed a few words with difficulty. She said words that had guided her over years, words that she had written with glowing letters – maybe not on her forehead but certainly deep in her heart: "Let us fix our eyes on Jesus..." In tears, I finished with her: "...the author and perfecter of our faith."[85]

The Biggest and Most Important Trip is the Hardest

Eva-Maria and I are so busy fighting Puschel´s illness that we do not really stop to think about the end. The 31st of January is simply another beautiful day with Puschel. And then all visitors are gone. Eva-Maria is preparing everything for the night as usual. We prepare the IV bags and pain meds together, the same as every day. As always, we stand by her bed and pray together. We are truly relieved that Puschel has been able to breathe calmly and deeply since the lung puncture.

Like most nights, Eva-Maria retires early to be able to do the early morning shift starting at 5 a.m. I go up to my office and watch Puschel every now and then on the monitor of my smartphone. For several weeks, we have been able to see Puschel through a camera from anywhere in the house. Puschel is sleeping calmly tonight. Around 1 a.m., I go to bed as well – of course not without checking on her once more. Her head has fallen to the side a little because we placed her bed at an angle so she could breathe more easily. I straighten her head carefully, hoping she won't wake up but instead will keep sleeping peacefully. This is the moment I see Puschel alive for the last time. Not knowing that this would be the last encounter, I go to bed.

---

[85] Hebrews 12:2. This verse is written on the wall over the altar in the chapel at Holsby.

When Eva-Maria wakes up very early as usual to check on Puschel, she returns to the edge of our bed shortly after and wakes me up with the words, "Hannes, our Puschel is now with our Savior." It is February 1st, 2012. Puschel's organs have stopped working completely. A few moments later, we are gathered around her bed. She is lying before us peacefully with a content, almost smiling, countenance. But she herself has been in heaven for a few hours already.

As we look at her – praying, saddened, everyone dwelling on their own thoughts – we are also a little relieved and thankful. Then we pray together, falteringly, and thank God for the life of our daughter and everything He gave us through her. She was a special gift from heaven. This does not take away anything from Puschel's siblings; they see it like that themselves.

She was a gift that was unique and, at the same time, a legacy that shaped all of our lives. We tell God all of this here by her bedside and ask Him to make her life a legacy for many of her friends as well – a testimony, an invitation to live intensively and decisively, focused on eternity. We continue standing there with thousands of thoughts running through our minds. Yes, God took her from us way too early. Why that is, we don't know yet. He surely does. I remember a verse from a Manfred Siebald song: "What we are holding in our hands so firmly is all just lent to us by God. We may manage it and shape it and give it back to Him."

Then I think of Job who, despite so much tragedy in his life, bowed deeply before God and said, "The Lord gave and the Lord has taken away; may the name of the Lord be praised."[86] To praise God, to have Jesus in our hearts and live with Him every day – that was Puschel's biggest passion.

Eva-Maria and I sit at Puschel's bed for a long time. Some of these thoughts we share with one another. Some we share prayerfully with God. And then the day dawns, with everything that needs to be taken care of. It is a nice day because it is shaped by thankfulness for everything God gave us – much more than it is shaped by sadness and questions.

---

[86] Job 1:21 [NIV]

Farewell

The doorbell rings around nine o'clock that morning. Visitors from Sweden are at the door. It is Puschel's friends, Donna and Wally, from Holsby, who were a little like surrogate parents to Puschel. They had let us know yesterday that they were coming; they had wanted to surprise Puschel. I smile sadly and tell them in English, "You came as planned, but Puschel is already with our Lord in eternity."

Only moments later we are standing by Puschel's bed. Just then, a ray of sunlight beams into the room, directly onto her bed. It looks like an angel is standing beside her bed. This is a good point to share part of a letter that Donna wrote to us right after the funeral:

> *Puschel was a personal encouragement many times! She had good reason to complain about her intense pain, but she didn't! She lived life to the full, above and beyond what would seem she was able to do. I was challenged in my own situation (back issues which eventually led to surgery) to "Give thanks with a grateful heart!" That was one of Puschel's favorite songs of praise. In 2008, Puschel sent me a poem she had written. She asked me to "edit" the English. More importantly, my heart was deeply touched with the simplicity of the poem and its message.*

> *Where do I step?*
> *Whose footprints do I step into?*
> *Who shows me the way?*
> *Am I walking blind?*
> *What is my goal?*
> *Am I alone on the way?*
> *My soul finds rest in God alone!*
> *He is my goal!*
> *And I do not go by myself!*
> *Peace and rest,*
> *Security and love,*
> *And abounding, never-ending grace.*
> *Without HIM – who am I?*
> *Gone with the wind!*

With HIM – I have everything that has worth!
Forgiveness forever!
My Friend, I want to be Your friend.
Be my Father!
Your child.

Oh the beauty of her life in Christ and that steadfast relation-
ship with HIM. She expressed it over and over again and her life
touched so many people – including mine!! I will always treas-
ure her friendship!!"

This February 1st of 2012 is an exceptional day in our lives. A day of parting, but also a day in which we are aware of the reality and presence of our God more than ever before. Wally, the Swedish-American friend, says repeatedly, "It is so beautiful to smell the fragrance of life instead of death." True indeed. There is calmness in everything – a peace "which transcends all understanding and will guard your hearts and minds in Christ Jesus." (Philippians 4:7 NIV). A little later, Grandfather Holmer and his wife come over. We sing songs and pray together and ultimately only praise God and thank Him for this fulfilled life, even though to us it seemed way too short. But as you know, God's clocks turn differently than ours. His thoughts and paths are higher than ours. (Isaiah 55:9). We are convinced more profoundly than ever that His Word is true and that His thoughts about us are always thoughts of peace. (Jeremiah 29:11).

The End of a Story on This Earth

It is with a poem written by one of her cousins that we want to slowly finish Puschel's story. It is God's story, which surely has no end. We are certain that much of what Puschel stirred in people on this earth will only be visible in eternity, for they are spiritual impacts which Puschel never took credit for but always ascribed to her faithful Father in heaven. You will be surprised in heaven one day....

What could I write about your story?
It is hard to say anything.

191

Your eyes, your smile – simply beautiful
It seems to be a fire that is not from this earth!
Fallen down, much has broken,
But you are still so strong
You run, you fight,
And you are always full of love.
So much is broken, you are often so exhausted
Over and over you experience it,
But you pray, are full of hope
You radiate this joy!
You say it would be okay if you had to go,
But you would also like to stay.
It is hard to express
How much you impress me,
What it means to me,
You impress me so much,
Many others as well.
You will be surprised in heaven one day
How many lives you have touched deeply,
The peace you speak about,
I feel it in your letters!
That peace within you can only be directly from heaven!
A star in the night, bright and beautiful.
Your light shines in the darkness.
It burns with the fire of eternity.
May HIS fire warm you.
May it hold your heart close through whatever happens.

Magdalena Holmer

This note was stuck to Puschel's Holsbybrunn journal from 2004. We do not know if it belongs to that period of time or later:

"Live as if today were the last day!" How would I live, if I knew that I "only" had one more day to live? What is the meaning of my life? What would I still want to tell certain people?

Now, I would think that I would be sorry for the people who are left behind. Because I am better off. I can look back thankfully on my life with God. Or did I still want to accomplish something specific? What would it be good for? For myself or for an eternal purpose? God, You gave me my life, and when You take it back, I still want You! I want to be a dawn of hope, an

192

encouragement for those who are afraid of death, because for me it is, I think, a celebration of joy to be with Jesus. And "only" for my loved ones will it be a funeral. But I wish for them to see God's path, accept it and make the best of it, which is telling people about how profound the joy will be in eternity! I cannot imagine yet what it will be like there, but I am also just a human being on this earth. "Teach us to number our days, that we may gain a heart of wisdom." (Psalms 90:12 NIV).

God did not perform the miracle we had hoped for. But it is a huge miracle, and surely the answer to so many prayers in those five years, that Puschel never questioned that God's plan is perfect. We can see so many paths in her life that a human being could have never planned. To this day, we as a family live by the knowledge that God answers prayers. That peace "transcends all understanding." We thank God and everyone who so faithfully prayed for Puschel and us over the years, and still do!

What I Learned from You

Puschel often talked about her mother, and during the last years she lived by her mother's dedicated and selfless care. Here is a glimpse of Eva-Maria's own thoughts, though everything written so far is absolutely felt and written by both of us.

It is a kind of letter to Puschel:

"When you came back home because of your illness, our live-stock increased heavily." That means, in concrete terms, to the two *donkeys were added a pony, a bunch of pygmy chinchillas, more and more chinchillas, cats and kittens, sheep, fish, and a horse. They, of course, all had offspring whenever possible. I actually always liked when our animals gave birth to their young. But the question of where to put all of the cute offspring did sometimes temper my delight. you usually disarmed me by a simple, `Oh, mom....´ And in your love language that meant, `Don't worry so much...!´ Your life motto always stood behind that: "God knows your past, give Him your present, and then He will take care of your future." So, I just joined in your joy....*

You loved the life God gave you so much that you just brought all life around you into your own. Because it was always a gift to you from your Heavenly Father, your Creator."

Farewell Service

During the farewell church service, Heinz Spindler, director of the Torchbearer center at Bodenseehof, talks about an encounter he had with Puschel. She had told him how easy it was to talk about Jesus with patients at the hospitals. She had also told him about the religious people who had interrupted our prayer when we prayed, Lord, Your will be done.

"It cannot be God's will that Lydia is sick. God's will is health, perfection and integrity," they said. Puschel's body wasn't healthy – yet this path was always God's path.

Heinz Spindler said that Puschel had asked him one day (probably rhetorically), "Did I do something wrong when I said, Your will be done? I have always only wanted that Jesus would use my life as a testimony for Himself. And He does do that when I meet with doctors and other patients."

Heinz Spindler writes:

I will never forget that statement of Lydia "Puschel" Holmer. I will also never forget Puschel's eyes when she said that. They were eyes full of hope and love for her beloved Lord and Savior, Jesus Christ. This has become an assignment and inquiry at the same time for me. This shall be my reason for life! There is no bigger statement for a Jesus-follower, no matter how young or old, and there simply is no better life fulfillment for a Jesus-follower.

I am forever grateful that Jesus let me get to know this young woman with her heartfelt trust in Him. May her life testimony help many people to find fulfillment, meaning, and hope for their lives. Most of all, I hope that this book may become what Lydia's life goal always was: "I have only wanted that Jesus would use my life as a testimony for Himself."

With unspeakable gratitude for those wonderful "Jesus encounters" through Lydia's life and that of her family ~

Yours truly, Heinz.

Epilogue by
"Opa Holmer"[87]

I have been deeply touched as I read the journal entries of my granddaughter, Lydia. I was amazed that a grandfather can **learn from his granddaughter - for instance, the simplicity of** her faith and confidence in her Heavenly Father. Or the certainty that God guides all things in a good and genuine way. There was also that deep peace when things turned out very differently than she had wished for. It seemed totally natural for her to lay everything before her Father – whether she experienced problems with other people or dealt with life's daily difficulties. And she had an enormous joy in God's wonderful creation. Apparently, she had amazing, continual conversations with her Father in heaven about that.

She calmly listened to her grandfather. Yet when he told her that she needed to work for a while (she had just graduated from nursing school), prove herself, and finally start earning some money, she firmly dismissed him. "But Opa, it is clear to me that I am supposed to go to the Torchbearers in Sweden," she simply said. And later she even cared for orphans and homeless children in El Salvador! Even a well-meaning, concerned grandfather could not deny this calm assurance. In hindsight, I now realize that this was probably exactly as it should have been. Lydia only had a little time, but she strove for a fulfilled life. It was a life filled with eternal wealth.

But where is the answer to all of our urgent prayers? God did promise that He would answer us. Many downright wrestled in prayer before God for her physical recovery. God decided differently. Multiple times Lydia herself wrote, "Father, Your will be done!" Seeing that, I just have to trust God that "His plan is perfect," and that He acted out of full love and wisdom regarding Lydia. He can run things in a better way than we could ever pray for. In eternity, we will realize that the one who is with Jesus does not want to go back.

---

[87] Opa is German for grandpa.

But can it be that God calls a young nurse away from such an important ministry to children on the streets and just takes it out of her hands? Yes, He can. Because since then, many things have also progressed at La Casa. Little houses are being built where the children live in families with house parents.

And Lydia's chapel bell calls them to hear God's Word. Meanwhile, her friend Myriam worked at La Casa de mi Padre with Daniel, her husband, and thus temporarily filled a void. Yes, they will go to a different country in Central America[88] for now, but God always fills the voids that people leave. Even though He doesn't need us, He does want to use us. He calls us to work and calls us into eternity.

A lot of things in this book are reported from Lydia´s father´s point of view. He was the one who primarily arranged the multiple therapy appointments as well as visits to the many places that his adventurous and mobile daughter wanted to see. Lydia's mother kept things running at home and warmly welcomed Lydia and her father when they returned. She was an indispensable and faithful caregiver – and not just during the last few weeks. It was because of her mother that Lydia constantly and inwardly longed to be at home. It is incredible how much love and strength can flow when a father and a mother stand together, pray together, and do what love demands.

Uwe Holmer

---

[88] Right now they are in Costa Rica

About the Authors

Johannes Holmer, born 1957 in northern Germany to
Uwe & Sigrid Holmer, has pastored in Mecklenburg since
1983. He is married to Eva-Maria Holmer.

Eva-Maria, born in 1957 in Dresden, is
a pediatric nurse and works actively in her husband's parish.
They have four children – one of them in heaven.